There is no Love
Without You.

finding You
in a world of It

By Rick Barrett
Illustrated by Micaela Colleen Barrett

Copyright © 2014 by Rick Barrett

Published by : Living Matrix Publications

www.rickbarrett.net
www.taichialchemy.com

Printed in the United States of America
First Edition:

Library of Congress Cataloging-in-Publication Data

ISBN 978-0-9960588-5-8

Cover design by Micaela Colleen Barrett

I am still learning from this very readable book. It is a uniquely rewarding page-turner. I have been part of part of the New Age movement since the sixties (when Abe Maslow personally brought me on board). I have written widely about it and now, from these pages, have begun to comprehend what it is all about. Here is the profound but lighthearted guide we have been waiting for. I invite you to join me on the adventure.

Lawrence LeShan, research psychologist and author of Landscapes of the Mind: The Faces of Reality

Here are words that will get you closer to the nature of it all than words have the capacity or right to. Based on many decades of seeking, grappling and finally synthesis, Rick Barrett has offered us an invaluable compass to the understanding of unity in a world of duality. Personal, witty, and with the gravity of felt experience, here is the story of all of us in the pursuits of one man. The symbiosis of inner and outer, Western and Eastern and ultimately universal truth in a digestible package is no easy feat. But here it is. Get nice and cozy with the great Mystery by Finding You in a World of It.

Abdi Assadi, acupuncturist and author of Shadows on the Path

I am always impressed when I talk with Rick Barrett and doubly so when I read him. His thought lies at the intersection of science, philosophy, mysticism, and the martial arts. And like the Tai Chi master that he is, he weaves them together with incredible dexterity. This book will challenge what you think you know about knowing and consciousness. It invites you to awaken to a higher level of consciousness—a participatory consciousness—that will greatly enrich your life. This book should not only be read, but lived!

Dr. Robert A. Delfino, Associate Professor of Philosophy, St. John's University, New York.

In *Finding You in a World of It*, Rick Barrett, the Tai Chi Alchemist, offers a groundbreaking reading of Martin Buber's philosophy, which makes Buber useful and accessible to the martial artist and to everyone else. A student of Rick's for many years, I have field-tested the invaluable techniques contained in this book in workshops, classes, and in my ongoing practice. I can honestly say that I would not be able to do what I do were it not for what this little manual makes accessible—now to the general public for the first time. Using anecdotes, stories, and easily repeatable exercises, Rick shows concretely that all of us can live fully present lives, both to ourselves and to those around us—starting now.
Read this book. Do the practices. *You* will change your life!

Rabbi Andrew Hahn, Ph.D., the "Kirtan Rabbi"

As a psychologist, I think that what Rick is presenting in *Finding You in a World of It* is a very practical level of stress science. He knows martial arts and how to listen. When we are able to listen, we can sense life's pressures and are able to deal effectively with the energy of each situation. We learn to yield, adapt, and creatively change in order to neutralize the pressure of the stressor. To be of service to others and help them to listen and to wake up.

Rick recalls his near-fatal fall as, "my intimate encounter with that concrete slab." There is a humorous, profound, Zen quality to that. We have to stop and say, "What just happened?" Fortunately, Rick recommends softer methods to the reader. He takes the essence of his martial arts to an inner art of being that encompasses everything in life.

> *Dr. John Beaulieu, N.D., Ph.D. author of* Music and Sound in The Healing Arts, The Polarity Therapy Workbook, *and* Human Tuning.

This book has become a daily meditation for me. Each time I re-read a section it takes on a deeper meaning. On the path of authenticity, *Finding You in a World of It* is a must-read! Barrett opens his heart and soul to share experiences and provide indispensable tools we can use to wake up to our true selves. This book is not an intellectual approach, but a down-to-earth body-mind-spirit discussion that will inspire the most spiritual as well as scientifically-oriented searcher.

> *Linda D. Addison, Bram Stoker Award author of* How to Recognize a Demon Has Become Your Friend

This book is dedicated to the visionary, Lawrence LeShan. His *The Medium, the Mystic, and the Physicist* was forty years ahead of its time. At ninety-two, he remains a beacon in the distance guiding us mere mortals to new possibilities.

Contents

Foreword

In 1989, on a 9-day Vipassana Meditation retreat, I suddenly found myself inserted fully and precisely in the exact arising moment, each moment separated by a gap. For one blissful week I lived Basho's haiku:

Old pond
Frog jumps in
Sound of the Water

It was a complete release from the routine commute between past and future into a succession of timeless "nows," a release that meditation alone seldom affords..

In the early stages of what became my life's quest to comprehend that blissful event I had the good fortune to encounter Rick Barrett. Rick, as it turned out, was also on a journey to understand a mystical experience, one that arose in the middle of a public event: a National Push-Hands tournament. In a most convincing, however unexpected, demonstration of the Tai Chi principle of *wei wu wei,* or "non-doing doing," he found himself so empowered by his full engagement with the exact arising moment that he "effortlessly" won the superheavyweight division. A middleweight had never competed as a superheavyweight, much less win.

Unable to account for it on his slow boat to the ancient wisdom of China, Rick made a critical detour: Martin Buber. Incorporating the seminal mystical text *I and Thou* with the *gong fu* of his own Tai Chi and healing practice proved to be an alchemical blend. Rick had not only found his way back to that that life-changing day, he had found the way to share it. His teaching evolved from the foundational "presence" and "wholeness" of Tai Chi's "body-mind-spirit integration," to the culminating stage presented in this book: "authentic engagement," or more simply, "meeting."

Rick's decades of probing and refining have all been in the service of one magical moment—a moment repeatable on demand, a thousand times a day. Through the years, I have witnessed countless students' amazed faces as they access this moment, a virtual re-creation of his super-human feat at that tournament. Frequently their startled look is accompanied by the same phrase: "But I didn't *do* anything."

Rick and I do not agree on the implications of that phrase, nor the deeper meaning of *wei wu wei*. I am a nondualist. Rick, with Buber, is not. But there is no disagreement that however individuated the "I" may seem to be, however *non* nondual, it has blissful lapses from that seeming. Had I not met Rick, and engaged the teaching that he has exquisitely set forth in these pages, I might still consider such lapses to be acts of "grace." Now I know that they can also be acts of "will," whatever the ultimate status of our will might be.

Jonathan Bricklin
Editor of Sciousness, *and author of* The Illusion of Will, Self, and Time: William James's Reluctant Guide to Enlightenment

Chapter 1
The Hollow Men

"**M**r. Barrett, please stand up."

The stentorian voice of my high school English teacher startled me out of my customary early morning stupor. Mr. McCoy was tall and handsome with a barrel chest, ramrod spine, and GI's buzzcut. As stern and resolute as an Old Testament prophet, he was as passionate about literature as I was lukewarm.

This particular morning he seemed intent on purging me of a bit of the folly I carried with me as a badge of honor.

"Mr. Barrett," he repeated, "it seems you are the only member of this class who didn't feel the need to complete today's assignment."

Oops. Major oversight on my part. This was one class where I knew I couldn't bluff or bullshit. My cloak of invisibility had been stripped away. All eyes were on me and I fully expected to be the subject of today's sermon.

What was that assignment? Oh, yeah…"The Hollow Men," Eliot's bum out poem.

Our dried voices, when
We whisper together
Are quiet and meaningless
As wind in dry grass

I could certainly relate to the "hollow" part...and the "meaningless" part too. It was stuff I had been wrestling with. But the only thing that mattered in this moment was avoiding humiliation. For a shy teenager, that is tantamount to tar and feathers.

Then something strange happened.

Mr. McCoy looked me in the eyes in a way I had never known. He dialed down his imposing presence and reached inside me with respect and gentleness, as if offering me an opportunity to get square. Or maybe he was doubling down, expecting me to implode. Time froze for a moment as I scrambled for a foothold.

"Perhaps then, in lieu of a written paper, you would like to share with us your understanding of the Eliot poem? Please take a moment to gather your thoughts."

I needed a moment, because a significant psychic event had just buffeted my adolescent consciousness. Something had shifted and I had no language for it. My rigid reality was melting like Dali's clocks. I wish I could say that the insights into Eliot that flowed from my mouth matched the intensity of my internal storm at that moment.

My comments weren't memorable, but (at least in retrospect) they probably weren't ridiculous either: something on the order of, "We don't have to be the 'hollow men'. There is more, and I'm feeling that now."

Eliot's words were a warning, not a sentence.

This seemingly insignificant event shocked me out of my lethargic indifference. I had just been impregnated by a sentient alien being. No, not Mr. McCoy. Something formless and unidentifiable had short-circuited my smugly dependable rational mind and transported me to another dimension.

I'm sure it wasn't apparent to anyone else. And it wasn't for many years that I would find words to make sense of it. How that teacher looked at me that day—directly into me, and communicating on an unspoken level—conveyed a soul-to-soul understanding and connection that I had never known.

Until that exchange—and it only took seconds—I had known only one way to be in the world: as an object among objects.

I was reasonably content with that way of existing. Everything could be named, numbered, categorized, explained, or described—including my own self. Since I was pretty good at all that, the deal was largely working in my favor.

Objectivity was tantamount to Truth, and I was certain that human beings could solve any mystery given the right information and sufficient intelligence. However, this little exchange with Mr. McCoy had shaken my faith.

A seed had been planted.

Where This Bus Is Heading

After thirty-plus years of exploring the paradoxical worlds of Chinese internal martial arts and energy healing, I have learned to translate and demonstrate much of what I have garnered for those unwilling or unable to immerse themselves so deeply. I'd like to share the fruits of my explorations with you. I hope you find them as enlightening and life-changing as I have.

Come with me on an adventure to Find You in a World of It. The view from there is quite spectacular. The You that we will encounter is not just another person we happen to be speaking to. It is the Eternal You that is beyond all form and limit, the You that awakens us to a world that is alive and responsive. Finding You inspires and empowers us to live and love and do things beyond our own self-imposed limits.

For the next few chapters I am going to lay the groundwork for practices that can bring these results into your life. It is important to recognize what I will be calling the "It-trance" and all the triggers that make that trance seem so indispensible. There are broadly held assumptions and patterns of thinking that stick us in the trance.

To even consider alternatives to the It-trance, we must unstick some of those adhesions. Like flipping a delicate crêpe with a spatula, we carefully disentangle the mental fusions a bit at a time until the mind is free enough to consider other options.

And the alternatives are actually quite practical.

As a martial artist and energy healer, I am prejudiced in favor of those practices that produce demonstrable, repeatable results. I like principles that are equally useful in neutralizing a punch to the nose, calming a rowdy class of fourth graders, and appreciating a Van Gogh painting or a Beethoven sonata.

I call the action of Finding You, "meeting." Meeting is like the electricity that powers my computer, television, and toaster: different appliances – same power source. Meeting makes everything work better.

Meeting does not happen independently of the "It-world," but in concert with it. You go beyond mere knowledge to actually encounter this living world and its inhabitants with your whole being. You return with lessons learned and stories to tell.

Some people do this quite naturally. Most of us don't. I had to learn how.

There are three primary elements that create the conditions for Meeting. And the presence and aliveness created by each of these elements are also themselves the wonderful fruit of the practice of Meeting.

1. **Coherence/Wholeness.** The human energy field is quite familiar to me. I work with it all day, every day. I know that when it is brought into Wholeness by your consciousness you are capable of so much more than you know. Effective power dramatically increases. The mind clears. There is less stress on your body-mind when your energy is coherent, and that means it doesn't wear out as fast. You are more intuitive and open to psychic phenomena.

When you are energetically coherent, you change your internal state to one that is calmer and more centered. There is less stress on internal organs. Balance improves. All this helps build confidence and optimism to participate in life, unhampered by fear.

And perhaps most important to the theme of this book, energetic coherence leads to the elusive body-mind-spirit integration that is necessary to shift out of the It-trance and meet You with full awareness.

What if we could learn to parlay moments of Wholeness into minutes? Hours? Days? Or at least be able to find that calm, powerful, alert equanimity any time we want?

What if it only takes a second or two to make the shift?

It does. And it's much simpler than you think.

2. **Presence.** Presence is conscious awareness of the moment you occupy. It's impossible to be fully Present when chasing the phantoms of what I'll be describing as the "It-mind." You must be able to shift from randomly channel-surfing your thoughts to controlling your attention.

Your ability to do anything is directly related to how Present you are and how well you control your awareness.

You are not your thoughts. They arise and disappear. Each has a beginning, middle, and end. There is a *space between thoughts,* no matter how packed they seem to be. Meditators practice for years to find the space between thoughts. You can learn to do it much faster. Really, really fast.

3. **Relating.** "When two people relate to each other authentically and humanly, God is the electricity that surges between them."

Martin Buber

When you relate, you resonate with another, soul to soul, and open to energy and information that is unavailable to the It-mind. You leave the safe harbor of objectivity to explore the sea of infinite possibilities. The You that is encountered is not just another object among objects, but a co-creator in a vibrant world. It is like the difference between observing a two-dimensional photograph of a lover and making love with the actual person.

In relating there is no fear. Only love.

Meeting needs Wholeness, Presence, and Relating. It requires being able to engage or suspend the It-mind at will. As impossible a task as this may seem, it is within your reach. Learning to meet will require understanding the It-mind and practicing the techniques in this book.

The good news? It's fun. And effective. And surprisingly simple.

The Long Journey to Find You

In my youth I regarded the universe as an open book, printed in the language of physical equations and social determinants, whereas now it appears to me as a text written in invisible ink, of which, in our rare moments of grace, we are able to decipher a small fraction.

Arthur Koestler, The Invisible Writing

It may be helpful to know a little about me and why I am so excited to share this information with you. My own path has followed an arc similar to the one Arthur Koestler describes above. I spent my youth comforted by the certainty that the universe would eventually surrender all its secrets to the diligent investigations of science.

Like Koestler, I too have been disabused of that idea, and have instead been led off the beaten track and into the world of Chinese internal martial arts, the human energy field, alternative healing, meditation, and consciousness research. All that has been tempered by the grounding effect of many years working as a carpenter, plasterer, and contractor.

For much of my life, I sometimes still felt like one of Eliot's stuffed men, mysteriously out of phase with what was going on. I was stuck in my head, but I hardly noticed. Everyone I knew seemed to be coming from the same place; we analyzed our own lives and loves with dispassion and detachment. Our "dried voices" were "quiet and meaningless as wind in dry grass."

Frustrated by this disassociated miasma of abstractions, I left college after a couple years in search of a more authentic life. I had no idea what that meant, but I knew I couldn't continue the way I was going.

Exquisite adventures, moments of ecstasy, and philosophical insights were lightning flashes that illuminated a night sky that quickly returned to jet. They did suggest the outline of something more, something that seemed to lead me on, but revealed no clear path. Two bright bursts shone brighter and longer, and affect me to this day.

While still a teenager, I once received a stack of books from the newspaper editor of the small western Pennsylvania town where I lived. The local culture at that time wasn't terribly supportive of original thought, but Bob Davis recognized a spark in me that he thought could be cultivated. He was a progressive intellectual in a town where conversations revolved around guns and bibles. He took me under his wing. We discussed literature and politics and would travel two hours each way to see experimental theater—plays like *Marat/Sade* and *Hair.*

In that pile of books given to me, there were works by Buckminster Fuller, Friedrich Nietzche, Marshall McLuhan, and other provocative writers. Among all the gems, one gleamed more brightly: *I and Thou,* by Martin Buber. I still consider it the most important book of the twentieth century.

Martin Buber

Martin Buber was born in Vienna in 1878. He considered himself a "philosophical anthropologist" and drew from diverse sources, including Hassidic mysticism, the Christian existentialism of Kierkegaard, German mystics Meister Eckhart and Jacob Boehme, and the philosophies of Hinduism, Buddhism, and Daoism.

He published his seminal work, *Ich und Du* (originally translated as *I and Thou*) in 1923. It is a challenging read. More than one person has confessed to me of throwing this small book at a wall in frustration.

My adolescent mind was unable to grasp the full significance of Buber's message, but it did awaken briefly from its trance. There was a Copernican shift in my worldview. Until then, I had perceived the world primarily through the filter of objectivity. The world was to be studied and analyzed, and I was certain that all mysteries would ultimately bow to the power of human rationality. This was the promise of several hundred years of scientific and technological advancement, and I rode that wave enthusiastically.

Buber opened my eyes to the possibility that there was another, richer way to be. It was a radical vision that took decades to assimilate, but forms the backbone of this book, my practice, and my life.

The second lightning flash happened after I left college and was employed as an ironworker in New Jersey. After so many years of schooling, I felt I needed to do something physical. It was a thrill to walk I-beams several stories up and to brave sub-zero temperatures. It felt "real."

But it was not where I needed to be, even if I didn't know it. It is said that Spirit speaks to us in the softest voice we'll listen to. If we don't listen, the quiet voice whispering in your ear turns into a tap on the shoulder and eventually smacks you upside the head. I needed that last method.

I ignored two bizarre mechanical failures where I could have been killed in my car. In one of them, my brakes failed in highway traffic, and I still don't know how I avoided a serious crash. I chalked it up to "Shit happens," and continued to plod along the path I was following.

It was only years later that I could see the pattern my life was taking. At that time, everything was still a random event in an impersonal universe. What was required was a voice loud enough to get my attention: I stepped through a hole in a roof I was working on and fell thirty feet onto a concrete slab. After I hit the ground, I tried to stand and reassure people that I was okay. I wasn't. My leg was broken. I promptly fell on my face and smashed my teeth on the cement.

The concussion put me in a coma for a week and I hovered near death. The doctors couldn't even operate to repair my broken bones and pull my broken teeth until it looked like I had enough juice to withstand surgery.

Thanks to the love and prayers of friends and family, I found enough impetus to fight back from death's door, despite the unbelievable pain. It was in that all-consuming torture that I encountered what it was to be alive and in the world, a glimpse into a different way of being. It wasn't that Rick was "feeling pain." Rick WAS pain!

There was no separate identity, no intellectual distance, just the relentless screaming klaxon of every cell in my body protesting and pleading for deliverance. The shock to my system was what I needed to get out of my head.

The agony subsided gradually over the next few weeks but my body became wasted and weak: my leg held together by a metal plate and screws in an old-fashioned plaster cast elevated by wires and pulleys, a hole in my mouth where a bunch of teeth used to be, and my broken wrist in a cast of its own. Doctors were pessimistic about a speedy recovery, although they said I'd be able to move around pretty well with crutches and cane for the next year.

When I was taken off morphine (against my wishes, I might add), my head gradually started to clear. My girlfriend suggested that I imagine a blue light flowing through my damaged limbs. As crazy as this notion sounded, I had little else to do but grumble about bedsores and being horny, so I gave it a try. My leg was hidden deep in its plaster sarcophagus and gave me no feedback, but I persisted nonetheless. This was my first contact with energy healing, and I had no map.

But there was something to it. Four weeks after my fall, I was released from the hospital, emaciated and atrophied. My legs were so weak I couldn't stand. But, six weeks after that, I was hiking on the Appalachian Trail in North Carolina, painting my parent's house from a twenty-foot ladder, and playing basketball (gently) with friends.

My recovery was happening four times faster than the medical professionals had expected, and some credit had to go to that mysterious blue light.

My brush with death had given me all the inspiration I needed to actually LIVE. I was filled with gratitude, no longer sleepwalking through life. I still had a long way to go, but at least I was wide-awake for the movie.

I had no idea what life had in store for me, but it now had my full attention.

The only offering you can make to God
Is your increasing awareness.

Lalla, Indian poet

Chapter 2
Getting into the Game

This is the real secret of life—to be completely engaged with what you are doing in the here and now.

Alan Watts

My intimate encounter with that concrete slab and the resultant traumas were a great awakening for me, but I had no idea to what. They ignited a passion to help others to live their lives more fully, even if I didn't know what that meant. I lacked the knowledge to understand the implications of what had occurred, and the experience to be of much help to anyone.

Buber's *I and Thou* and my puzzling encounter with the mysterious healing blue light had opened me to new possibilities. Clearly my neat little worldview was not expansive enough for this new phase I was entering.

I wish I could say that the turnaround was immediate. It wasn't. It took decades to start living a life I could consider authentic. The path was labyrinthine and filled with cul-de-sacs. I was looking for authenticity in a time when "get real" was code for get a job and forget your dreams.

After ten years of nibbling at the edges of what I later came to understand as body-mind-spirit integration, I heeded the call of practicality and submerged myself in running a construction company for fifteen years. It was a fun game for a while, but then the soft whisper again turned into a shrill siren and I got "really real" and moved on with my life's work. My long detour into contracting crashed and burned and I realized I had stayed way too long.

I felt the pull.

I was practicing self-taught acupuncture on my employees (surprisingly successfully), teaching Chinese internal martial arts (primarily t'ai chi ch'uan) and practicing energy healing while putting in long hours in my business. These were empirical practices that explained, demonstrated, and effectively utilized the abilities and phenomena that some consider paranormal. The "healing blue light" I had utilized after my fall turned out to be but one way of using consciousness to affect the energy fields of the body-mind.

What kinds of phenomena? There are many examples: A small woman easily holds back the force of a large weightlifter; a soft touch of the hand sends a large body flying; I cradle someone's foot and their headache evaporates; point a finger and anxiety disappears in seconds; people sense energy fields in each other from a distance.

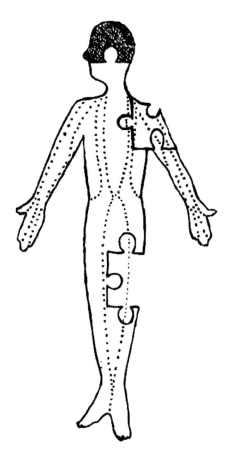

"Affecting the energy fields of the body-mind"

I wasn't satisfied with the conventional explanation for such things. Simply labeling them wasn't the same as understanding them.

My first book, *Taijiquan: Through the Western Gate*, explains how some of those things are not only possible, but also predictable and teachable. But when people witness an event that goes beyond what they consider to be "normal," there is a natural skepticism. We tend to reject the anomalies, even when they are staring us in the face. Santayana wrote, "The empiricist...thinks he believes only what he sees, but he is much better at believing than seeing."

That is because we are limited by our beliefs. They are the foundations we rest upon, but also the walls of our prisons. Blake called them "mind-forg'd manacles." *Self-limiting beliefs* have the wonderful advantage of always being "correct." My mother would often meet my negativity with, "Argue for your limitations and they are yours."

If you believe that humans are just ambulant bags of water powered by chemical processes, for instance, then you will probably have trouble trusting healing practices, like acupuncture or polarity therapy, that place emphasis on the human energy field.

Scientists actually measure some of the energies in the human field with mechanical devices, but it is still a jump to consider that they can be controlled by our thoughts and actions. Even when the t'ai chi master or the energy healer demonstrates some remarkable ability again and again, doubt still remains. You don't want to be tricked into believing something that isn't so, but you can also be fooled by disbelieving what is.

Sometimes it requires temporarily suspending some of your beliefs when the facts no longer fit the theory.

One thing that energy medicine and internal martial arts have in common is that they slow things down...way, way down. T'ai chi exhorts its practitioners to, "Find the stillness in motion. Find the motion in stillness." In a craniosacral therapy session, I may hold someone's head for the better part of an hour, tuning into the cranial rhythms. I notice things that are invisible to someone rushing through.

The most important lesson I learned from decades of slowing it way down is that the magic comes from conscious, focused *participation* with your whole being, not by just showing up and taking notes, nor by amassing a storehouse of techniques and information. You have to involve yourself in what you are doing, willing to be transformed by it. In participatory consciousness we can access abilities and information that are not available when we are detached from what is going on.

Do you have a memory of being so involved in something that you didn't care how you appeared to others? You were challenged to show your A-game and you delivered. Nothing else mattered. There could have been a sense of "timelessness" and enthusiasm. Maybe you were playing a sport and were "in the Zone." Or you were painting or writing and everything worked so perfectly it almost seemed effortless.

The Zone fits in with psychologist Mihaly Csíkszentmihályi's explanation of the *Flow* state. In Flow, one is completely immersed in an activity with an energized focus, and there is a good balance between the perceived challenges of the activity and one's perceived abilities.

To be in the Flow state you must have a clear idea of what is going on and what you are trying to achieve. There is a sense that the activity is intrinsically rewarding. Often there is an absence of reflective self-awareness.

Full participation with one's whole being runs counter to our very human tendency to immediately fit each experience into our ongoing narrative. All that matters in Flow is the game being played, not how I can represent it to others.

"The ability to objectify"

However, the ability to objectify events and organize them into meaningful thoughts and systems of thoughts is one of our most precious skills as humans. We separate out from the moment to tell a story about what is going on, even if only to explain it to ourselves. Our minds fashion an abstract model so that we can fit the events into the larger picture of our lives. Doing so shifts us into *non-participatory consciousness:* we are outside of the event looking in.

This process is really fascinating, and we'll look at it in more depth later. For right now, just consider that we can't both watch the movie and be in the movie at the same time without doing a really poor job of both. Often, we are watching the movie of our own lives—and narrating in our own heads—instead of actively participating.

In *Taijiquan:Through the Western Gate*, I wrote about how this objectification takes us only so far. The "Western Gate" in the title is a metaphor for the limits of scientific materialism and the philosophies it spawned, and is a gate in that it blocks as well as grants entry to realms beyond it.

The Western Gate is a profound milestone in human development. A huge debt is owed the courageous pioneers who demanded that knowledge be based on rational investigation and empirical experimentation. In challenging ecclesiastical authority and dogmatism, Western science and philosophy made an important leap forward in human evolution.

This rationality became the foundation for the huge strides we have made in transforming our planet into a global (if frequently contentious) community. It provides us with an ever-expanding array of tools for understanding and interacting with our world.

Yet this metaphorical gate remains locked to those who can only think objectively. The vast territory beyond is invisible and inaccessible. To the guardians of the Gate, it is assumed that rationality is the *ne plus ultra* of human consciousness, and that a human computer that can think faster and store more information is the ideal.

This perspective structurally limits them to a view of the surfaces of things, never their depths. A world visited by artists, poets, mystics, and lovers lies just beyond, but can't even be seen through the locked gate.

Scientism is the elevation of *scientific materialism* (the assumption that all phenomena can be explained scientifically as a product of matter and energy) to the status of religious dogma. Its true believers are convinced it is the one true faith. It derives its validity from its brute power to explain certain phenomena in its own terms in a predictable way. Credence is given only to that which can be described and/or quantified. Success is judged by measurable results, and this is precisely what exalts the Western Gate.

Objectification/abstraction has been around since humans could think, but never has its dominion been so extensive. That is because science-based industrial culture is so good at what it does. Not only does it get spectacular results, but the Western Gate is also very good at justifying itself as the dominant paradigm in the world today. It imposes order in the rich chaos of Nature…and has the statistics to prove it.

The story told by the Western Gate casts itself in a most favorable light because it owns the primary language being spoken, as well as most organs of communication. It moves boldly forward, navigates through its rearview mirrors, smugly explains the phenomena that has already passed, and makes predictions based on patterns it observes. This way of thinking protects and comforts us against the piercing light and the penetrating darkness by translating the world order into an ordered world. But at such a cost!

Living in a world where we objectify everything does not ultimately work best. In record numbers, people seek chemical intervention to remedy an intractable negativity. According to a Wall Street Journal report (November 16, 2011), the use of psychiatric drugs rose 22% between 2001 and 2010 in the U.S. One in five American adults now use antipsychotic, antidepressant, anti-anxiety, and ADHD medications. In some cases, this is just what is needed to turn things around. For others, though, the drugs themselves become a problem.

Prolonged use of any powerful psychoactive chemical is likely to have unforeseen consequences as well as the litany of known risks recited in the drug commercials. That so many millions of people are willing to roll the dice gives testimony to the importance people place on shedding the widespread gloom that infects so many of us. Who doesn't know someone who depends on a prescription to keep them in the game?

It's time to know that the game can be played differently. Heroin, cocaine, crystal meth, and a wide assortment of designer drugs are as prevalent as ever. Teenage girls cut themselves. Internet gambling, pornography, and shopping create new addictions.

The more profound our abstractions become, the further we distance ourselves from the lived life. But can we do both? Can we distance ourselves from events to contrast and compare, to develop systems of understanding (and systems of systems), and also engage life and the world with love and enthusiasm, immersed in this moment as though there were no other?

Isn't this what it means to be human—to play the game and be able to think about it too? Most of us are living that way already to some degree, but confusions about what to do and when cause us to drive with one foot on the gas and one on the brake. And that's a rough ride! Let's smooth that out a bit by identifying our options and how to shift between them.

An eye is meant to see things.
The soul is here for its own joy.

Rumi

Chapter 3
The World of It

Truth is not a fixed point; it is not static; it cannot be measured by words; it is not a concept, an idea to be achieved.

J. Krishnamurti, Indian philosopher

Finding You in a World of It.

Finding *You* in a World of *It.*

Say those words to yourself a few times. For many of us, a kind of healing begins just by hearing or saying them. We intuit that there is way too much *It* in our lives, and far too little *You.*

We feel oppressed by the roles that we and others assume in the games people play. It is easy to fall into fixed patterns of behavior and relationship, and sleepwalk uncomfortably through life.

All power and meaning seems to originate from the Its—money, position, sex, fame, thrills, prestige, and even science, religion, and philosophy. So the solution for many is to get more of whichever "It" it is that seems to scratch the itch.

The World of It can be a hollow, lonely place when it is the only place we know. It is a world of surfaces, not depths. It is the world of objects and only objects.

When you are deep inside the World of It you may feel you are in a "dog-eat-dog world." A dangerous place. It lacks heart. Devoid of soul. You feel alienated and alone. All you see are objects. Even people are objects. Many appear dangerous. You find it difficult to connect with anyone in a fulfilling way. A trick of the mind turns every person that you meet into an It. And that turns *you* into an It as well.

This "world" is familiar to us all, and arises anytime we engage in the indispensable human activity of making sense of what is happening. We objectify everything and tell ourselves the story of it all.

I say the world "arises" because the It-world is a mental fabrication and comes into being only when one of us sentient creatures identifies something. It includes every *thing*. For many it is the *only* world. It is the world of stuff—objects. Of science and technology. Knowledge. Sights and sounds, words and thoughts, and in the words of Lewis Carroll, "of shoes—and ships—and sealing-wax—of cabbages—and kings."

Whatever we can think, name, quantify, imagine, or dream about is part of the It-world.

It is a "world" because when you are in it, you have the sense that it is *all there is*. To think otherwise is often disregarded as a silly waste of time. Yet there are limits to this worldview, limits that are not easily seen when the alternatives are disregarded. But when our world collapses into a purely mechanistic one, it loses its depths and becomes a hollow world of illusion.

The "objects" I'm referring to are not just apples and cars and galaxies. Ideas can be objects too. And they can be denser and harder than granite or titanium.

Whenever we focus on the qualities or characteristics of anything or anyone—no matter how ephemeral—we must objectify to do so. There must be an object of our attention—an It. We can only think about something when we separate it out from the cosmic bouillabaisse we all float in. It becomes an object of our attention.

But is representing and thinking about the life we live the same as life itself?

In the It-world, that is the case.

There is an alternative, however—a way of being in the world that is not based on objects. We all have known such states of being and have visited there often. It happens when "I" meets "You" in reciprocity—not attempting to use or manipulate or categorize in any way.

I meet You, not It.

For example, frequent riders on New York City subways will habitually avert their gaze from strangers. In a crowded city, they must be choosy about whom they interact with. Occasionally, though, eye contact will be made and the stranger won't look down immediately. In that moment, the two strangers can choose to meet each other as sentient beings, perhaps even acknowledging with a smile. Nothing more need be made of this exchange, but in it their humanity was understood and acknowledged.

"Mowing the weeds of It"

Such encounters are quite common, but often so ephemeral that the chatter of the It-mind easily overwhelms them. They are like beautiful, delicate flowers that appear in every garden, but often go unnoticed when surrounded by the fast-growing weeds of It. Before we can properly examine this I-You relation, we will have to cut back the weeds a bit by clearly identifying the mechanism of the It-mind.

Finding You in a World of It is essential for an authentic life. "You" is not an object, even if the *experience* of you (lower case) is as an object.

There is a subtle distinction here that changes everything. It is an entirely different way of being, one with the power to transform and enlighten. Until we do consciously encounter You, we walk in shadows: objects amidst objects. We collect names for objects and construct theories about them and adroitly manipulate them, but even if we amass knowledge, power, and fortune, these treasures are empty and hollow until we can relate to others non-objectively as well.

Jeremy Boob, a character in the Beatle's "Yellow Submarine" movie, was created to illustrate their popular song, *Nowhere Man.*

He's brilliant in a way, but lost in his own skewed analysis of the life that he studies but never actually lives. Trapped in the World of It, he is so fascinated by categorizing phenomena that he is oblivious to human interaction and the moment-to-moment wonders of the lived life. He's miserable.

We all know some people who are Nowhere Men. And there are also people who somehow sense there is more to life. They long for the I-You relation.

Many people despair of ever finding a heart-to-heart, soul-to-soul connection. They fill their lives with vanities and distractions, and when the emptiness oppresses too much, they inflict pain upon themselves and others. They fill themselves with experiences to give their lives meaning and excitement, yet it is in the very nature of *experience* that their problems begin.

To experience any*thing,* the mind must identify it as an object to be experienced. And you, the experiencer, are objectified as well. (Common use of the word "experience" actually traps us in the It-trance. This will be discussed at greater length later.)

But is that the only way to be in the world?

Would it be of any value to have moments—or even extended periods of time—of pure Presence, and then also be able to shift quickly into peak performance? Aren't there moments when you are so involved in what you are doing that the apparent separation of subject and object are dissolved? Are moments of openhearted connection with another person only rare, serendipitous events—or can you feast on them heartily and often?

Maybe you have answered those questions for yourself. We have all had glimpses, and some of us engage life with robust enthusiasm. But when we try to share our insights with others, how often the words perversely take us in a different direction.

Our well-intentioned attempts to bring order and meaning to life solidify into self-limiting beliefs. We embrace an ideology, religion, or philosophy as "true," then use it to filter out and disregard anything that doesn't fit. Those who wear rose-colored glasses prefer to see the world as optimists. Cynics assume selfish motives underlie all actions. Both seem to experience the world they expect to find.

The It-world has become so dominant in our current time that the alternative is marginalized, if it is known at all. It is a trance-state so pervasive that even our language acts as a trance-induction that takes us deeper and deeper. We may awaken occasionally, but are pulled back again and again by our own words.

It is the ultimate catch-22. We have to use words to describe what we mean, what we feel, what we experience. Somehow I have to use words here to explain what I mean by that which is beyond experience—what I mean by I-You. But the very act of using words puts us in the It-world.

Remaining awake requires examining and understanding that words forge the bars to our prison. We have to go beyond the words, the objects, the experience, and into something more profound than language can express.

"Use words to get beyond words"

Paradoxically, to share this way of being we must use words to get beyond words, keeping in mind their power as well as their limitations. Language itself cannot take us out of the It-world. Too many booby-traps. But carefully examining our self-limiting beliefs can help us see where those ideas prevent us from seeing the mountain right in front of us. Then you can choose to climb that particular mountain or not.

Of course, simply recasting a debate that has been ongoing for thousands of years into new terminology is not going to get the job done. That is just rearranging the furniture. Transforming object-based consciousness requires *participation.* You can't just think about it. Or talk about it.

Participatory consciousness is essential to experience the richness and fullness of the lived life. *Non-participatory consciousness* keeps it at a distance.

Beyond the Western Gate

The World of It is created by *non-participatory consciousness.* That is, you separate out from something to think about that thing, thus suspending your participation. Like vacationers who insist on videotaping every minute of their visit to exotic locales, you can spend all your time looking at your life and precious little participating in it. This way of being is habitual and sub-conscious, and we rarely notice how deep it goes.

My daughter Micaela was sitting in Washington Square Park in Greenwich Village when a large hawk brazenly appeared, apparently unfazed by the hundreds of people engaged in various human activities. The hawk soared through a jazz quartet, skimming their heads with its huge wingspan. Micaela's astonishment at seeing this large raptor in the heart of New York City was quickly interrupted by the awareness that she was *already narrating the event to herself.* She had unconsciously distanced herself from the event. This is non-participatory consciousness: narrating the event back to yourself as it is happening. We are all too often videoing or watching through the cell phone camera to "capture the moment," instead of simply participating in that moment that we hoped to record.

To break out of the It-trance, Micaela told herself, "Wait, you don't have to tell me what is happening. I'm HERE. I'll catch up on the story later."

Our story is important, but life is in the moment. It is in only the present that we participate. We are authentic then, unarmored by the filters of abstraction. When we "experience," we do not participate in the world. Experience is always between us and our thoughts. The world is uninvolved in that exchange. Whatever we think about has already moved into our past.

To pass *through* the Western Gate is to embrace the *Mystery.* It is to leave our thoughts of the past for the eternal present. We let go of the predictability of a crystallized known and knowable for an unimaginable vortex of potentiality. To go beyond the It-world is to embrace What-is, knowing that it can be participated in but never used, encountered but never known, embraced but never grasped.

We can pass through the Gate, but must return—again and again. We need the It-world to survive, but those who know only the It-world do not really Live. Anyone can pass through this gate at any time, but those entranced by the It-world do not remember having done so. A moment spent in the land beyond is labeled as just another experience and is stuffed into the closet with all the others.

For example, an emergency demands that a small woman perform some extraordinary feat. (The classic example is lifting a car to save her child.) She must shift to full participatory consciousness immediately—without equivocation. In that state she embraces the Mystery, the Field of All Possibilities, and is able to do something unimaginable. She leaves the crystallized known and knowable for an unimaginable vortex of potentiality.

Later she tries to understand what she experienced in language she knows, terms acceptable to the Western Gate. "I was so scared that the adrenaline took over." It is a neat little story now, with an acceptable chemical moral to it, and she has forgotten her visit to the Mystery. She is comfortably back in the It-trance.

Even a dramatic event like this can be dismissed as just another experience, another story. It is much easier to ignore the vast, unordered potentiality of the Mystery.

George Santayana wrote, "Experience is a mere whiff or rumble, produced by enormously complex and ill-deciphered causes of experience; and in the other direction, experience is a mere peephole through which glimpses come down to us of eternal things."

Our "glimpses of eternal things" pull back the curtain to reveal the eternal in each of us. Our finite experiences give our lives feeling and meaning. Finding You in a World of It opens the gate between the eternal and the experiential, and allows us free and safe passage.

*One particle of dust is raised and the great earth lies therein;
one flower blooms and a universe rises with it.*

Chan Buddhist text

Chapter 4

The Trance of Objectification

This life's dim windows of the soul
Distorts the heavens from pole to pole
And leads you to believe a lie
When you see with, not through, the eye

William Blake

What stops us from feeling really good most of the time? Why is it so rare? Why is it often so hard to create the conditions that warm our hearts and uplift our spirits, even when we know that is what we desire most?

The Stoic philosopher Epictetus wrote, "Some things are up to us and some things are not up to us. Our opinions are up to us, and our impulses, desires, aversions—in short, whatever is our own doing."

If that is the case, Mr. Epictetus, why are so many people anxious and depressed so much of the time? Is there more to it?

Sometimes a pleasant memory or a smile from a stranger is all that it takes to get you back on track. But if your funk is deeply imbedded, the problem goes deeper. Even those of us who don't feel particularly depressed may have a prevailing unease or lack of joy in our lives. We feel out of resonance, out of tune, out of phase with life.

This book is about awakening from the powerful *It-trance*, the Trance of Objectificaton, which is as old as the human mind. Awakening enables us to live an authentic life.

Writing about such a trance is difficult because our language was born of the trance and its use reaffirms it. There are tripwires everywhere capable of triggering emotionally charged verbal booby-traps that plunge us into old programs that no longer serve.

The trance of objectification draws its power from that most human of abilities: the making of stories. We are fascinated with our own story and with the stories of others. And the BIG STORY ("What's it all about?") provides steady work for philosophers, scientists, and the clergy.

Some are willing to kill or die over disagreements about the telling of a story. Myths arise in every religion to bear witness to how special their guy is, and to lend credence to the specialness of his particular message. Fundamentalists, dogmatists, and ideologues of all kinds proudly proclaim that their story is the special filter through which they perceive life. And they are perplexed that you and I can't see something so obvious. History is filled with examples of "true believers" willing to torture others to make their argument a bit more persuasive.

We become en-tranced when we confuse our story with what actually IS. Stage hypnotists demonstrate this power when they sell a story so well that their subjects enthusiastically wear underwear on their heads or engage in public shouting matches with their private parts. Politicians use story to manipulate their constituents to support (or at least acquiesce to) questionable laws and programs.

Wars are sold by propaganda designed to objectify some group of people as an enemy. Humans have a hard time waging war against other humans, but will do so against an enemy. An "enemy" is not an actual person, just a dangerous object.

Objects. Its. It-world. It-trance.

The Map and the Territory

It is the mind that gives to things their quality, their foundation, and their being.

Buddha, Dhammapada

The trance of objectification kicks in when we identify too strongly with the products of our minds—our thoughts—and confuse them with what is really going on. We confuse the map with the territory.

Maps are representations of that small part of the world that we can describe at any given time. Alfred Korzybski, Polish-American scientist and philosopher, wrote, "Two important characteristics of maps should be noticed. *A map is not the territory it represents,* but, if correct, it has a similar structure to the territory, which accounts for its usefulness. ... If we reflect upon our languages, we find at best they must be considered only as maps."

Language is a map. Language is not the territory. It uses symbols and noises to represent the territory. Our words are maps and allow us to communicate complex ideas.

Real-life experience has to be objectified into symbols that take the place of things and ideas. Symbols have the advantage of portability, which comes in handy when talking about things like rivers and elephants and nuclear non-proliferation. They can be combined to express complex ideas, and even ideas about ideas (as I am doing here).

Most of what is occurring in any moment is beyond the awareness of any individual. The tiny piece that grabs our attention in any moment is filtered through a nervous system designed to give us only the headlines about what is going on. From that paltry information we construct our ongoing narrative.

"Illusion of furniture"

For example, I was once in an artist's loft with a crew of carpenters. Beside the entry door stood a wooden chair. At least I thought it was a chair. One of the carpenters put his coat on it. When the artist came into the room, he freaked out. "That is NOT a chair! That is an art piece!"

It was actually *papier mâché*, painted to look like a chair. The artist's story was very different from the carpenter's or mine. If a fly alighted on it, most likely the question of its "chair-iness" would not occur to the fly. A toddler might see it as an unidentified object among a roomful of unidentified objects. Each of us would have different understandings of what that object was, based on our interactions with it and what we knew of the back-story.

Whatever was in that room before I encountered it was not yet an It for me. It became a "chair"—for me—when I interacted with it. It became a faux chair when I interacted with its creator. Which was it? At this reading it exists for you, the reader, only as an idea communicated by words on a page. It exists for me as a memory.

Whether we express an idea in language, or just think about something, it must be objectified. That is, the multi-dimensional totality of what is being considered must be flattened and trimmed to fit into a word or group of words.

For instance: a puppy. No matter how descriptive, creative, or poetic I am with my word choices, I can never materialize the furry fleabag on the page. I can only provide some hints to jog your memory of puppies you have known. Or, if you have lived a puppy-deprived life, compare it to something familiar to you.

Words are maps, and "A map is not the territory." A map is only valuable if it represents the territory accurately. The confusion of the word with what it represents is a source of much of human suffering. The labels we put on things can become more real and more important than the thing itself. To be known as "Johnny's girlfriend" is more important to some than whatever it really means to actually be Johnny's girlfriend.

Advertisers, public relations people, political campaign advisers, and trial lawyers all know how important it is to use the right words to spin things favorably for their clients. The symbols can even take on more reality than what is actually symbolized. Sorting through the confusion of words, and what the words represent, is a path to wisdom. To use our maps effectively, we must be able to read them correctly.

Modern science brilliantly maps much of our physical world. Some of its principles can be extended to the much more complex and mercurial world of living creatures, but doing so requires flattening them like cartoon characters. Objectivity requires that life be expressed in terms of surfaces only. It maps some aspects of the world so well that we can be forgiven our eagerness to extend this brilliance to all human interests. However, objectivity confuses the map with the territory it represents. The map becomes more important than the territory.

"If it walks like a duck, quacks like a duck, and looks like a duck… it's a duck." This example of "common sense" is often the trump card played when establishing what "really" happened. The implication is that things are as they appear and should be labeled thus. And this approach is essential for a rational, scientific understanding of events. It is a helpful approach to establishing agreement among people about what is going on.

If you and I can't agree about the duck, then it's hard to establish trust about other things. But if a whole bunch of us agree about the duck thing, then we have a "fact." That enables us to get our stories lined up in a workable way. It can be quite reassuring to get others on the same page, even if the duck we agreed on eventually turns out to be something else entirely.

For instance, if you and I stand on a beach on a summer day and see the sun in the sky, that sun is a "fact" to us and we respond to it as such. We ignore for the moment that the sun that we are seeing is actually an image from about eight minutes ago. Scientists tell us that this is how long it takes for light from the sun to reach us (another "fact"). But it's cumbersome to factor that into the conversation: "Wow, that sun from eight minutes ago is sure hot today."

Our reality is based on our shared perspective, and so you courteously don't correct me by saying that the sun is actually the same temperature as it is in wintertime.

So we just agree about the duck and get on with it.

Is anything really as it appears? One step beyond the Western Gate lays the entrance to a world *beyond appearances*. And things get progressively stranger the farther you go. Navigating that world requires a different way of thinking.

The actual "objective" appearance of things is something that does not exist—or rather, it exists as data that is literally infinite in its complexity and subtlety. What assuredly floods in upon the retina is an amorphous chaos of visual stimuli into which the human eye learns to inject a favored order of some sort or other.

Patrick Heron, painter

Chapter 5
Things Are Rarely as They Appear...but That's OK

Words are but symbols for the relations of things to one another and to us; nowhere do they touch upon absolute truth.

Friedrich Nietzsche

Dao (Tao), the Absolute, Suchness (Tathata), Ground of Being, Brahman, Parabrahman, and God—these are a few of the names given to that which is beyond words, the Mystery. Each has its own rich tradition and metaphysical implications. The discussion at hand (Finding You in a World of It) could easily bog down if bound too tightly to any particular ideology. Any term could call up centuries of debate and challenge.

But we don't need to know the ultimate nature of everything to agree to call whatever is going on in any moment *"What-is."*

The term What-is is pretty neutral. Whether you consider that everything is some form of matter and energy *(materialism)* that will eventually yield to scientific investigation *(scientism)*, or that it's all an embodiment of mind *(idealism)*, or some combination of the two, "what is" is still...*What-is.*

Simply put, *What-is is the event prior to its being thought about.*

Physicist David Bohm and philosopher J. Krishnamurti in their *The Limits of Thought* discussion agreed to start with that as their "duck." Said Bohm:

We have to be careful because the language continually tends to put us in separation. We tend to think that "what is" is reality and that truth would only be correct knowledge about reality. But what we are proposing here is to turn it around to say that truth is "what is," and reality as a whole is nothing but appearances.

Bohm and Krishnamurti's simple starting point is essential to understanding the It-world. *Truth* is What-is. *Reality* is not What-is. Reality is how What-is appears to us, and what we think about it.

What-is is the actual event, and reality is what we agree that we think happened.

Drawing a distinction between what is happening and what we *think* is happening starts to unstick the glue that holds the trance together. This

may appear to be hair-splitting to some, but having a neutral, easily understood term like What-is permits a conversation, regardless of philosophical or religious beliefs. A distinction is made between what is going on and how that event is experienced. (Don't worry if this takes some time. Even the great Krishnamurti had to be corrected by Bohm when he confused the two.)

This point is colorfully demonstrated by mentalist Derren Brown in a stage show. He placed a banana on a pedestal on the stage in full view of the audience and explained that sometime during the performance a man in a gorilla suit would walk across the stage and take the banana. After a while he asked the audience if they saw the gorilla. Most were surprised that the banana was now gone. Only a handful said they actually noticed the event—a man in a gorilla suit walking on the stage and taking the banana—despite it occurring in plain sight. The audience's attention was on other events taking place on the same stage, so they were not conscious of any banana-plucking gorillas.

Video replay confirmed it though. The event—What-is—included a man in a gorilla suit walking across the stage. The *reality* was very different for most of the observers. Their experience did not coincide with the event, despite being told what was going to happen. Some version of the event, as well as an awareness of having been tricked, was now *real* to them.

Their reality changed with information that altered or contradicted their previous story. What-is didn't change. It is still What-is.

What-is includes a lot of things dressed in gorilla suits. Our minds can never see all of them. Our senses provide millions of bits of information each second, but only a tiny fraction gets the attention of the conscious mind.

Probably for the best. Too much information would freeze us into inactivity. Rational thought reduces the aperture through which we view What-is to a manageable level. Thus we label things and compare them to other things and concoct useful explanations. To think about anything, an event must be converted into a mind-object, an abstraction.

What-is is the unique, infinite, continuous, seamless, unbroken Wholeness that is Now. It cannot be explained, envisioned, or imagined any more than a photograph of a crowd scene can replace the human lives depicted. Yet we try. It is our nature to try to explain what we can, even if all we can come up with is, "God works in mysterious ways."

Hans Vaihinger wrote in *The Philosophy of "As-If"*:

It must be remembered that the object of the world of ideas as a whole is not the portrayal of reality—this would be an utterly impossible task—but rather to provide us an instrument for finding our way about more easily in this world. (Emphasis his. Note that Vaihinger uses the term "reality" as I am using "What-is.")

I call any attempt to explain or depict What-is a *story*. (This paragraph is, by that definition, a *story*.) Vaihinger called such attempts "useful fictions." The small part of What-is that captures our attention at any moment I call an *event*.

What-is. Event. Story. These are not conventional philosophical terms. Why not stick with jargon that is more familiar, at least to philosophers and metaphysicians? After all, the conversation has been going on for millennia.

It is mainly for that reason that a simpler terminology is used here. Philosophical jargon has accumulated a lot of baggage in its journey, especially when translated into different languages and imported from different cultures and eras.

For example, I tried using the Chinese term *Dao* for What-is. Respected Daoist scholar Livia Kohn translates the opening lines of the *Dao De Jing:*

The Dao that can be told
Is not the eternal Dao.
The name that can be named
Is not the eternal name.
The nameless is the origin of heaven and earth;
The named is the mother of the myriad beings.

Seemed pretty clear to me. But after reading a few hundred different translations of the same passage, it became apparent that using the term *Dao* would bump up against the many different meanings that people assign to it. I could not reasonably appropriate the term for my own purposes.

What-is gets to the point without having to examine its metaphysical underpinnings. There is a minimum of assumptions. The term doesn't limit or describe in any way. It merely allows us to talk about that which can never be fully expressed by language.

Where's Waldo?

There is a series of children's books published in the U.S. as *Where's Waldo?* (*Where's Wally?* across the pond) by British illustrator Martin

Handford. You open the book to a large picture made up of small illustrations of people engaged in a wide variety of activities, usually around a central theme (circus, zoo, and the like). Your eye initially encounters an unintelligible confetti of squiggles and colors. As you narrow your focus, however, you recognize the illustrator's intention to depict amusing activities and encounters...dozens of them.

Your mission is to find "Waldo," a specific character in this teeming stew of humanity and goings on. He's tall and wears a red-and-white shirt, a funny hat, and glasses. Seeking Waldo drives your interest in exploring the tableau and gives meaning to the pages in front of you. Many events are happening simultaneously, and to bring your attention to any one of them requires filtering out the others...for the moment. The events on the page are not "objects" until you bring your focus, identify them, and make sense of what is happening. When you start to assign meaning to these squiggles and colors, you construct a story. Prior to the story there is What-is.

If you've ever played golf on an autumn day, you know about constructing a narrative from a visual kaleidoscope. When you crest the hill scanning for your little white ball amidst a gazillion fallen leaves, you are already prepared with your expectations. You have a sense of where it may have landed and how far it might have carried after that. You know that the colors overwhelming your visual cortex are leaves in the final chapter of their journey, and that your ball may be hiding under any one of them. Sense impressions are organized according to your intention to locate your little buddy. And that intention derives from an awareness of the game you are playing.

What you perceive is largely driven by what you are looking for.

If you pass by the same field with no knowledge of golf, the little white ball may not even exist for you. You are involved in an entirely different game (walking the dog, perhaps) and you see this impressionistic landscape with different eyes. The dimpled white sphere could be sitting on top of a pile of red and gold and brown and yet be invisible to you.

It is not part of your story, so it doesn't exist *as an object*. If it is anything, it is an undefined, unperceived part of What-is. If another golfer discovers it later, it becomes an object again—in a new narrative—as a "found ball."

"*The Treachery of Objectification*"

Its *object-ness* comes from being thought about.

French surrealist Rene Magritte painted a pipe and beneath it was the caption, "*Ceci n'est pas une pipe.*" ("This is not a pipe.")

The title of the painting is *The Treachery of Images*. In this and other works, he playfully emphasized how the words and images used to represent something are so often erroneously confused with the thing itself.

Our stories are not bad things in themselves...far from it. They are essential to an orderly existence. To survive we must have some idea of who we are, where we come from, our personal history, what is important to us, and who and what our allies and our enemies are.

All human knowledge comes from our attempts to get the story right. To do that we must think about It, talk about It, write about It. What-is must be made into an It to become "real." It becomes more real to us when we get agreement about it.

As long as we remember that reality is not what IS, but only how it *appears* to us from a particular perspective, we maintain a sane relationship with what is going on. When the story and *What-is* are fused together (con-fused) we enter the It-trance.

We lose ourselves in the World of It.

Finely or broadly articulated, we each, at each moment, have a world picture. Generally, we are not aware of what it is, but it is always present and determines much of what we perceive and how we act.

Lawrence LeShan, psychologist

Chapter 6

Finding You

If I know what love is, it is because of you.

Hermann Hesse

I first met Brian when we were both quite young. I was twenty-three and ill-prepared for the responsibilities of parenthood. He was but a couple of minutes old and fully absorbed in learning the fundamentals of mouth-breathing. He emerged from an arduous and dramatic Easter Sunday entry into the world with the desired number of fingers and toes and a substantial nine pounds, ten ounces of body mass.

The obstetrician and nurses had seen it all before, of course, and they performed their jobs with the detached professionalism one expected in 1974. Babies had been coming into the world for quite a long time, and they had seen their share. The doctor gave a perfunctory slap to get the newborn howling and quickly snipped the umbilical cord. A nurse wrapped him in a blanket and brought him to me.

"My reality was different from theirs"

My reality was different from theirs. Nothing could have prepared me for that moment. This was not just another birth among billions.

My heart exploded and I was no longer a child myself. I knew three dimensions when I entered that room. There were more now, and I had no words to explain them.

All the clichés you hear about your encounter with your first child suddenly had fresh meaning. I took him securely in my arms, looked him in the eyes, and began to speak. "Hi. My name is Rick. I am your father. You mother is Kay. You are in a hospital in New York City and it is April 14, 1974. You have a new body and a new life. We have named you Brian. If you don't like that name, you can choose another later. We will do our best to take care of you until you can figure out how to do it for yourself. We are very happy that you have come to us."

Brian immediately opened his eyes, stopped crying, and smiled. There was a sense of mutual recognition that was bigger than all the other events happening around us. Like, "Hello, Old Friend. It's so good to see you again." A portal to a new world opened for us and a bond was formed. Something happened between us that words cannot contain.

In that moment, Brian was not "my son" or a "newborn baby." He wasn't even "Brian." Those are all labels. And as convenient as they are for sharing information, a label can never replace the thing being spoken about. No, Brian was not just this new human object that displayed the familiar qualities that identified him as a person. Brian was YOU.

It was not an I-It moment. It was I-You. We connected. Soul to soul. The world was no longer neatly divided between "self" and "other." That boundary dissolved into wonder. Nothing else mattered. In the moment of our meeting, I found You in a World of It...even if I didn't know it at the time.

That is what I meant earlier when I stated we all have had times of I-You, even if we didn't recognize it as such.

Getting more of that I-You relation is the purpose of my writing... to live an authentic life, whatever form it takes. To be and know Love. And when I encounter You with my whole being, I am authentic and true. I know Love.

Buber put it this way:

Every actual relationship to another being in the world is exclusive. Its You is freed and steps forth to confront us in its uniqueness. It fills the firmament—not as if there were nothing else, but everything else lives in its light.

Hide and Seek

What does it mean to "find You in a world of It?"

It's actually something we all do, and have done, since we were infants. One of the first games we play with children is peekaboo where the whole purpose is to "find You."

With babies, we disconnect briefly by hiding our eyes behind our hands, pretend the child has disappeared, then re-connect and say, "Peek!" Baby laughs and wants to play more. In the moment of "finding," *You* are all that matters, and "everything else lives in Your light."

Older children play some variant of hide-and-seek. I am the "It" seeking a hidden object, until I find You. When found, it's your turn to become "It" and I become the object being sought. It's an archetypal game that is universally echoed in movies, literature, and popular cultures. Alan Watts said, "I have suggested that behind almost all myth lies the mono-plot of the game of hide-and-seek."

It is not an exaggeration to say that these simple games can become an opportunity for spiritual awakening. If I can put aside all the distractions that claim so much attention during an ordinary day and meet some person with my whole being, it is magical. In those moments, I step outside the world of objects and encounter her in the purity of her being.

The It-world is the world of objects. In it, everything appears as an object, including all humans.

The It-mind renders the vast, multi-dimensional orgasmatron of existence into a cropped, flattened, and edited version that a finite intellect can appreciate. It is how the world looks from the outside. Most of what is happening is beyond our awareness at any given moment, but it gives us some comfort to focus on those things we believe to be true.

We label things and shift awareness from the things themselves to the labels we attach to them, and to the inferences we make about them. Budweiser is no longer the cold, bitter liquid in the aluminum can; it is now the "King of Beers!" "Sauerkraut" was renamed "Liberty cabbage" in the U.S. during World War I. Zealots unsuccessfully tried to re-label "French fries" as "Freedom fries" in 2003 when France refused to back the invasion of Iraq.

The reality changes with the labels and our reactions to those labels. What-is has not changed. Finding You takes us beyond the labels.

Finding You is a simple thing, but far from trivial. Its simplicity belies its power to awaken us from a dream where we are forever looking through the patisserie window of life, noses pressed against the glass, seeing the delicacies within...but never tasting them. Finding You takes us *inside.*

Fast forward a generation from Brian's birth, and his six-month old daughter Kiara sits in my lap. She erupts into peals of laughter when she looks me in the eyes and sees me seeing her seeing me seeing her... she thinks that is the funniest thing ever. Her whole body quivers with joy. I am transported in that same moment and our shared laughter fills the room. It is the only thing going on in the whole world. No sense of separateness. Touching soul-to-soul. She is not my "granddaughter" (an abstract role) in that moment, but my partner in the eternal dance that transcends all form. We resonate together in a way that dissolves the boundaries between us.

"We resonate together in a way that dissolves the boundaries between us"

Children often find it easy to relate in this way. The world has not yet calcified for them. They talk to their stuffed animals and dolls as if they were living, intelligent beings, not mere figures of cloth and plastic. They relate to imaginary playmates, and feel different when they do— liberated from the expectations of others, full of possibilities. More important, they feel connected in a lonely, uncertain world.

When I connect with something or someone, life *is* different. I am no longer talking to just my mind—my ideas about you. I am talking to...You. I don't observe you or think *about* you; I stand in relation *with* You. We resonate together in the present. No story. No agenda.

When we encounter another in this way, the You that is invoked is unique. There is only one You. This You is no mere object among other objects—something to be labeled, experienced, and thought about. No, when we meet with our whole being, *You* are exclusive.

This is baffling to the It-mind that sees only you and you and you and you—as objects that we are talking to, audiences for our soliloquy.

Why just ask the donkey in me
To speak to the donkey in you,
When I have so many other beautiful animals
And brilliant colored birds inside
That are all longing to say something wonderful
And exciting to your heart?

Hafez, Persian poet

Chapter 7

Our Dual Nature

God turns you from one feeling to another and teaches you by means of opposites, so that you will have two wings to fly—not one.

Rumi, Persian poet

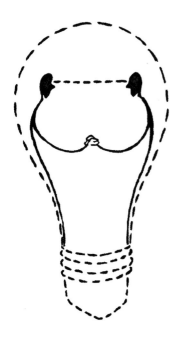

"The electricity that surges between them"

Finding You is not just another experience. In fact, it is not an experience at all. It is the helium in the red balloon of experience: invisible, lighter than air, lifting us to the heavens. In its purest, most profound expression, finding You has the potential for blissful, transcendent spiritual awakening. It can be a rapturous, soul connection that says, "Nothing else matters in this moment but You!"

Buber said, "When two people relate to each other authentically and humanly, God is the electricity that surges between them."

For many, the spiritual element is more than they could ever hope for, and Buber's I-*Thou* only has the loftiest context for them. But when his *Ich-du* is translated as "I-You," it has a more mundane, practical aspect as well.

It may be found peeking through many layers of contrivance and artifice, like the performance of a fine actor who brings new light to oft-repeated lines. It may be in the glance of a stranger at a convention, or the wisecrack of the waitress who serves your breakfast. And that is where it finds its balance with the indispensable It-mind to improve functionality in the lived life.

Our dual nature is the essence of our humanity. Neither aspect tells the whole story, but both are useful in explaining what it means to be human. The It-mind allows us to map our world and tell our story. Finding You enables us to embrace our fellow creatures as co-participants. Both are essential to a full life.

For too many of us, there seems to be no alternative to a third-person view of self and other, a subject-object frame of reference. We may awaken occasionally, but are pulled back again and again by our own words.

Two Operating Systems

It is useful to consider our dual nature as two different operating systems in one computer. An OS (Operating System) enables the machine to translate computer codes into actions it can perform. Two popular ones (at this writing) are Microsoft's Windows, and Apple's OS X.

They process data in very different ways, and a program specifically designed for Windows won't run on an OS X operating system. It's not as if they just understand different languages where things have different labels. They actually process information in ways that are unrecognizable to each other.

To run any program on a computer, you must boot up the appropriate OS. Neither can recognize programs that are not designed for it. (This analogy may not be so useful at a future time when all computers can understand each other's codes, but it works for now.)

When I think about something or someone, I am activating the operating system of *object-based awareness.* This OS organizes on the basis of qualities it can recognize. It is a way of being in the world that we are all familiar with. We have been using this operating system since we were infants. Attention selects an item or items and temporarily ignores everything else.

Let's call this the *I-It OS (I-It Operating System).* I-It views things from a subject-object perspective.

When I use the I-It OS, I know that everything must be expressed in *objective* terms. I can only see people and things as objects. I even recognize myself as an object. That's okay, because when I am using this OS, it is ALL about the story anyway.

In this mode, *I* am a thing among other things. And all of us things have qualities, and sometimes we can be named, and counted, and talked about, and written about…all the cool stuff we've been able to do since we developed brains big enough to abstract the bits and pieces of the world. (I-It can also be "Me and Him" or "Me and Her," where both me and the person spoken about are regarded as objects. For brevity's sake we use I-It to describe any such objectification.)

I-It is just fine for most of what we do. It permits us to bring order, meaning, and predictability into the world of phenomena. Science is the purest use of this OS. It crosschecks itself by demanding that an idea must be tested before that idea is accepted as a fact.

This is usually done by comparing the idea to what can be observed (appearances). Only those ideas that have been tested by qualified practitioners using the appropriate protocols are considered valid. Stories told in the language of science are pretty reliable, at least from that limited perspective. Only a small part of What-is can be understood in this way, but it can be quite useful. Usefulness is the major selling point for the I-It OS.

In fact, I-It is such a powerful operating system, we can easily forget that there is this other OS, one in which OBJECTS DO NOT EXIST.

We will call this the *I-You OS.* It is the operating system of *relation* and permits us to consciously resonate with someone or some thing. If I could ask the I-It OS if I should boot up the I-You OS, it would probably answer, "Are you kidding me? That one can't even see the obvious! It just spouts nonsense."

Buber calls I-You *relating.* I-It he calls *experiencing.*

In moments of pure relating, there are no objects. No story. In I-You, we relate to others as fellow sentient beings, not as objects.

Whole being to whole being. When we do that, there are no objects. There is only Now. We are together in Now, part of the seamless fabric of What-is.

To clarify, *Now* (uppercase N), as it is used here, is not something that can be observed or quantified. It is a statement of the relationship between one's awareness and What-is...*before the story kicks in.* That means that I must be aware in the moment I am actually in, not in some narrative about some other moment. I am Present (uppercase P) in objectless awareness.

When I am in the I-It OS, I focus on myself as an object dealing with other objects. Let's use the conventional lower-case *now* and *present* for what can be observed and quantified as objects. "Martha is here *now.* There are fifteen students *present.*" I-It.

All experience occurs in object-based awareness. Buber explains that we experience things only as they appear...as we sense them. To experience anything there must be some separation between the experiencer and the experienced. In the I-You OS, that separation is narrowed and replaced by a sense of resonating together. At its purest, all abstraction dissolves, replaced by a non-objective knowing.

Of course, humans are not computers and this talk of operating systems is an analogy. It does serve a purpose, however. Visualizing a dual nature of complementary operating systems can be empowering in a way. It reminds us that we are not our thoughts, nor their servants. Attention can be directed in ways that make our lives more fulfilling. We can learn to activate the appropriate operating system to enhance performance, understanding, inner peace, and transcendence.

Calvin and Hobbes

It is the spirit of the age to believe that any fact, no matter how suspect, is superior to any imaginative exercise, no matter how true.

Gore Vidal

"People are recognized as aggregations of qualities"

Many of us have used the I-It OS for so long that it seems the only way to be. People are recognized as aggregations of qualities. They are tall or smart or Japanese or atheist or female or athletic or neurotic… whatever they appear to be from our perspective. We recognize them by their attributes.

When encountered by someone who meets us with her whole being, we often don't know what is going on. There is something different about her that we can't fit into our usual thinking. She meets us as You, not just another character in her script. And she would like to be met as You as well.

This You may appear to us in many forms: parent, sibling, mentor, or lover. Or pet, forest, ancestor, saint, or angel. (You does not have to be human.) Socrates had his *daimon.* Rumi had Shams.

And Calvin has his Hobbes.

The difference between the two operating systems is illustrated brilliantly in Bill Waterston's long-running comic strip, *Calvin and Hobbes.*

To Calvin's parents, Hobbes is just a stuffed animal. When we see Hobbes from their perspective, the tiger is clearly an inanimate object. And Calvin is their perplexing and sometimes vexing son. They have no insight into his vast inner world, and must rely on his unpredictable behavior for clues. In the World of It, we can only know the surfaces of things—how they appear. We know Calvin's parents that way, too. They say and do things that we can understand.

When Calvin engages Hobbes as You, however, something miraculous happens. We enter the complex, exciting, magical inner landscape of a boy who says You to the best friend imaginable. Hobbes is not just a figure of cloth stuffed with cotton. He is infinite potentiality. He opens the gates of wisdom, compassion, responsibility, and play. He also excites Calvin's boyish rascality and daring. Together, they try anything and everything and learn life's lessons through their shared adventures.

It is easy to dismiss this living Hobbes as a product of Calvin's vivid imagination. While accurate in a way, that label misses the larger point: From time to time, each of us must meet the world and its inhabitants with our whole being, not as abstract components of a story but as fellow participants in the cosmic dance. (And there is only the *story* in the World of It.)

When we think *about* something, we must do so at a distance. To the degree that we resonate together, there is no such separation.

In Hobbes, Calvin connects with the one entity that gets him in the fullness of his being. The tiger loves without limit or reservation. In his friend, Calvin finds You. As he matures, he will most likely learn that Hobbes is a stuffed animal, an It among other Its. But he may also learn to find You in the humans, animals, plants, and things in a world of infinite possibility.

Another boy encounters a tiger of an entirely different stripe in Yann Martel's delightful novel, *Life of Pi*. The shipwrecked teenager, Pi, survives 227 days in a lifeboat with a Bengal tiger named Richard Parker. Pi awakens spiritually as he reaches with love, compassion, and understanding toward a creature that considers him the ultimate It—lunch.

Like the It-mind, Richard Parker sees his traveling companion as an object to be used. Pi transcends his own terror through love and opens to adventures unimaginable to a mind that cannot find You. He accepts Richard Parker for what he is and embraces his own dire situation as well. The story that emerges is quite different from the dismal one his It-mind suggests.

Love at its purest has no agenda. It does not possess or exploit. It embraces people and things exactly as they are, not how we want them to be. Our darkest fears disappear in the light of this love. The It-mind organizes its information differently when sustained by it. Solutions appear where none existed before.

Love does not exist without You.

*If I speak in the tongues of men and of angels, but have not love,
I am only a resounding gong or a clanging cymbal.
If I have the gift of prophecy and can fathom all mysteries and
all knowledge, and if I have a faith that can move mountains,
but have not love, I am nothing.
If I give all I possess to the poor and surrender my body to the
flames, but have not love, I gain nothing.*

1 Corinthians 13, New International Version

Chapter 8
Operating the Operating Systems

We are each of us angels with only one wing, and we can only fly by embracing one another.

Lucretius, Roman poet and philosopher

Okay, we know that you are not a computer and that those two ways of encountering the world aren't really "operating systems." That idea is a "useful fiction," as Vaihinger might call it. Just as it is useful to know the difference between wakefulness and dreaming, it also helps to consider these two different modes of existence.

In *The Medium, The Mystic, and The Physicist*, research psychologist Lawrence LeShan calls object-based and non-objective awareness "Sensory Reality" and "Clairvoyant Reality," respectively. He writes:

In the pure *state of Clairvoyant Reality, for which some mystics strive and which some say they have achieved, all specific content and all events and subpatterns vanish. This, however, seems as hard for most of us to conceive of as a* pure *Sensory Reality state with unique events and no relationships.*

Thus, there are two ways of perceiving and reacting to reality; both potential in man, both necessary for his fullest existence, his fullest potential.

Our default mode of existence is to objectify everything. It is the preferred OS in our culture. But there is that non-objective mode, too. Both are essential for a full life.

When you can consciously shift from the I-It, then you can access the I-You. You can spend more time in *relation*. You will see what I mean shortly when I take you through an exercise so you can alternate at will.

It is a simple idea:

In an object-based mindset, everything is an object.

In a non-objective state, there are *no* objects.

This is not a new idea and can be found in the great Daoist classics from over two thousand years ago. By making the distinction between I-It and I-You, Buber showed us how to enter the non-objective state: by engaging someone with your whole being.

To a mind only familiar with object-based, representational thinking, the I-You state may seem strange and distant—maybe even impossible or unattainable.

It is not.

It is actually nearer to you than your own breath, and something we all do and have done since we were infants. When we stop constructing our story for a moment and actually engage someone, we *relate* to him or her in a special way.

This is not the diluted, neutered version that often passes for social intercourse, or even the fixed roles and expectations of what is commonly called "a relationship." Relating is what happens when you look someone in the eyes and see them as conscious beings...*whether or not they return the favor.* (Yes, you can relate even if they don't. More on that in later chapters.) You recognize something special in them in that moment that reminds you that there is indeed a ghost in the machine.

When you and I relate to each other fully, there is rapport, communion. When I say I-You to something or someone, I change. I am no longer talking just to my own mind, my ideas about you. I am talking to... You.

I feel different. I don't observe you or think about you; I stand in relation with You. We resonate together in the Present. No story. I step out from the Trance of Objectivity and find myself firmly in Now, wide awake.

This takes some getting used to, of course, like eyes acclimating to bright sunshine. We may not get it at first, but with practice we start to notice some subtle but important things. A martial artist or athlete will pick up on an opponent's intention well before they show anything physically. A mother will sense her child is conflicted or upset. Senses are sharpened, and paranormal abilities may pop up unexpectedly. Synchronicities—meaningful "coincidences"—become common.

Energies and information will be accessed that are unavailable to the It-mind.

Social Conventions

We have a choice in each moment between I-You and I-It, even when we don't realize it. We can also learn to move rapidly and smoothly between them in the course of a conversation. That takes practice.

Social conventions can make practicing difficult. This was even more the case in Buber's time. In a world where you can have a thousand Facebook "friends" who all know whether you prefer boxers or briefs, it may be odd to consider that one could offend another by using the wrong personal pronoun.

But in early twentieth century Germany, such things mattered. It was considered rude to speak to persons using *du* unless you knew them very well. The more formal *Sie* was proper. A colleague corresponded with Buber for five years before he felt it appropriate to ask permission to address him as *du*. *Du* conveyed a level of intimacy and trust that had to be earned. It also said, "I wish to communicate to you person-to-person, not as the roles we perform."

The French also have this convention, and use two forms of "you," depending upon the level of intimacy: *vous* and *tu*.

To awaken from the It-trance we must buck up and prepare to address another as You—conscious being to conscious being—regardless if we know them well or merely bumped into them on the street corner.

The following exercises will help you to get started. Try them now. Try them for yourself. I-It feels different from I-You, emotionally and physically.

Exercise: Feeling I-You and I-It

Exercise 1.

Have a person or persons speak about you while in your presence. Looking away from you. As if you were eavesdropping. Something neutral, like a comment about your hair or shoes. Notice what it feels like to be talked about.

Now have one of them look you in the eyes and speak directly *to* you (not at you). Even if the information is the same, the two ways of communicating contrast. For example, "His shoes are brown," and "Your shoes are brown." When you are being talked about, the separateness is easily seen and felt. Resonance increases when you are spoken to in a way that honors who you are. You feel affinity for the speaker. Reverse the roles where you become the speaker. Notice what you feel in these two modes.

Exercise 2.

Talk about yourself in the third person. ("Rick is sitting as he writes this. He pauses and takes a breath. He shapes the next sentence in his mind." You get the idea.)

Notice how you must separate out from yourself to objectify to that degree. I-It applies even to oneself.

Now speak to yourself as You. ("Hey, you're doing a good job. Why not take a short break and stretch out. I notice you're a little stiff from sitting in one position." You are still conveying information, but via the I-You OS.)

To be self-critical we must objectify ourselves as an It. We construct a self-image that is imperfect in order to discuss those imperfections in our own head. Sometimes we use abusive language we would never use with a person we cared about. ("You idiot! What do you think you are doing?") Chapter Sixteen shows how to escape from the downward spiral of self-bashing by interrupting your narrative.

But objectifying your self need not be disparagement. When we talk about self-image, we are discussing *ego* and our relationship to it. Ego is a minefield of its own and deserves its own discussion. Far from being a demon or an enemy, ego is simply "self as an object." We'll discuss how to make ego a powerful friend in Chapter Thirteen.

Two Important Qualities

As you become more familiar with these two modes of existence, two things become apparent:

1. *There are no thoughts in I-You.* We enter a state of consciousness *beyond* thoughts and *beyond* separateness. Usually these moments are sandwiched unnoticed amidst our more familiar I-It thinking. If we can shift attention to addressing a partner in this dance of I-You, we enter the space *between* thoughts—clear and undistracted in the present moment. This clarity is often very brief since our thoughts can appear to be a constant stream. Experienced meditators are familiar with the space between thoughts.

2. *I-You only exists in the Present; I-It only in the past.* Objective time and space are products of experience in I-It, and in I-You they are replaced by a new time and space defined by the very act of relating.

For example, who hasn't spent time catching up with an old friend only to be surprised that hours have passed? You know there was some duration, but it doesn't always coincide with your perception of clock time. You know there was space, but it wasn't much bigger than that occupied by you and your friend.

The world went away for a while. Sure, there were thoughts popping in and out, but they were less important than the pervasive rapport that made the time you spent together something very special. Experience was interspersed with relation in a higher proportion than was the norm, and that lifted your spirits. You were more present and less concerned about other things.

Another example: Imagine spotting a girlfriend you once cared deeply about at a reunion. Could it be her? It's been so long. But it looks like her. (All I-It language.) You go over to talk and a big smile of recognition comes over her face. Reciprocity! You dissolve into a big hug. Nothing else matters in the moment but you and your old friend. There is only *Now* and *Here*. I-You.

It is not just with people. We can enter I-You with a beautiful passage of music or a brilliant dramatic performance and the rest of the world disappears. It is like standing before some jaw-dropping vista or a beautiful painting. It can be a magical moment. Then someone says, "Isn't that amazing!" and instantly we move from I-You to I-It; from relating to that beauty to *thinking about it*.

It is inevitable to shift from I-You to I-It as we try to make sense of the moment. Fortunately, a new moment of magic and beauty can be found by restoring I-You again and again.

It takes practice to shift freely between I-It and I-You. The first step is to become aware that it is possible.

I-You in the Ordinary

I-You happens in our daily lives, but often through the safety of established social rituals. They provide acceptable forms for our interactions.

When we meet an acquaintance on the street, we ask "How's it going?" or "How are you?" Our primary purpose is not to learn information but to establish contact in the here and now. We are saying, "I care about you enough to ask about your well-being" (even when we don't actually want to hear all the details). Each meeting is an opportunity to crack through the It-trance and make authentic contact with another person.

A traditional greeting in India is *"Namaste."* It literally means, "I bow to you," but has come to mean, "The Divine Presence in me greets the Divine Presence in you." This ritual of greeting very clearly emphasizes relation over experience. The I-You relation does not last, but each time we go there we glimpse (however briefly) the timelessness of greeting another, soul-to-soul. Then, even when we return to experience mode, we may still feel the radiance generated by our brief mutual recognition.

Too often, people allow their perceived lack of social skills to restrict their interactions with others. Or, we may greet others perfunctorily, reciting our lines without actually interrupting our own inner dialogue. Communication of all kinds can be excruciating to some, and they may go to great pains to avoid any contact. "What do I say? I don't want to sound stupid."

Small talk is a social convention that helps us bridge our separateness. "Nice day," "Think it'll rain?" or "Did you see the Super Bowl?" are universally innocuous gambits that provide opportunities to engage others. The purpose of such lightweight conversation is not to exchange information, but to create a safe space for I-You. Once established, we can move to weightier topics if we like.

People love pets because they can move easily into I-You with their furry friends. They can speak all kinds of silliness to a dog or cat without a worry about how they are perceived. There is reciprocity. When my cat sits in my lap and stares into my eyes, it is clear that all she cares about is that moment of connection. When my dog eagerly greets me at the door after I have been away, all that matters is the relation we are both feeling.

It is in our I-You moments that we know our Wholeness.

I am fond of pigs. Dogs look up to us. Cats look down on us. Pigs treat us as equals.

Winston Churchill

Chapter 9

Experience and Beyond

Out beyond ideas of wrongdoing and rightdoing
there is a field.
I'll meet you there.
When the soul lies down in that grass
the world is too full to talk about.
Ideas, language…even the phrase "each other"
…doesn't make any sense.

Rumi

What is the biggest barrier to awakening from the Trance of Objectification?

Words.

The very things that free us can trap us as well.

Words frame our understanding and provide context for our

perceptions. They can also tell us what to perceive and how. "Chilean sea bass" is more appetizing for most people than "Patagonian toothfish." Same fish, different name. Hypnotists, poets, advertisers, and mothers all know the power of words to transform perceptions.

Some words form the

bedrock foundation for our worldview. They shape the way we live our lives. "Experience" is one of them.

For the many who only know the World of It, everything that one does or says or thinks about is an experience. That would include relating. To an object-based consciousness, relation is just a subset of experience. It's another thing you do and think about and create a story about. People even talk about mystical, "non-dual," or transcendental experiences as though they were cut of the same cloth as eating dinner or watching a movie. Those exquisite moments actually take us beyond experience, but do become "experiences" when we recall them.

Experience is a fuzzy word for a lot of us. The term has become a catchall to include whatever is going on. But just because something is happening somewhere it doesn't mean that it is part of your experience. An important qualification (for the word to have any meaning) includes *the direct observation of or participation in events as a basis of knowledge*. It comes from the Latin *experientia* (to try, to prove) and is related to "experiment." It contrasts with thinking about or imagining something, and its many definitions include the sense of being personally involved in the event.

When used as a verb, *experience* is always transitive. That is, we experience some *thing*. There is always an object being experienced, some point of focus. That "object" need not be solid, perceptible, or even "real." It can be an idea or a hallucination or a dream, provided there is some *thing* that the mind can focus on. All experiences are finite. They have a beginning, a middle, and an end. And you are there for the event.

A key part of experience is being personally conscious of what is happening.

Events are happening constantly, but each of us can only be aware of an infinitesimal part of What-is. There are also events that you are aware of, but not conscious of. (You can be aware of dozens of conversations in a crowded restaurant but not conscious of what any of them are actually discussing.)

To be conscious you need to know something is going on—and know that you know it. Experience begins when you fit the event into your story somehow. That's one of the jobs the nervous system does for us. It sorts through tons of information, discards most of it, and comes up with a short fragment that our conscious mind can digest. And that takes time. Thus, ALL experience occurs in the past.

That's right. ALL EXPERIENCE IS PAST EXPERIENCE. By the time an event registers on your nervous system, you are already in the next moment...even if your mind is still trying to sort out the ones that are already gone.

What is a moment? It's when consciousness takes note of some part of What-is.

There are moments when there is no finite point of focus, or even a sense of self—moments that we later describe as timeless, infinite, or transcendent. Awareness is expanded

"Archiving past experience"

but non-directional. Such moments may be interpreted later as spiritual awakening or even a descent into madness, depending on your personal and cultural frame of reference. Some have attempted to label them as "direct experience" or "non-dual experience," but that seems to violate the very nature of the word "experience." Like a colorless rainbow or dry water.

I don't consider it helpful to simply label moments of objectless awareness as "just another type of experience." The label disguises the major shift in mode that is occurring. It's okay to talk about a "non-dual experience" after the fact. What one remembers of the event is converted into a narrative, and the event's objectlessness becomes a story with a beginning, middle, and end.

For example, you encounter a breathtaking vista or sunset. There is a moment prior to the mind's recognition of what it is that is being perceived (like the confusion of colors and squiggles on a page of *Where's Waldo?* prior to the construction of a meaningful explanation of what is going on).

That is the moment of What-is. By the time we can react and say, "Wow! Isn't that amazing!" a small part of What-is has become an object for us. We have moved from relating to what is going on to experiencing how it appears.

Philosopher Jonathan Bricklin explains that ancient Greeks held that humans walk backward into the present moment. They could only see what has already gone. Poet Samuel Taylor Coleridge agreed, "To most men, experience is like the stern light of a ship, which illumines only the track it has passed."

In *The User Illusion,* Danish science writer Tor Nørretranders shows the limits of the conscious mind. The "user illusion" in the title refers to the interface between computer and user. The "illusion" that we see on the monitor is a short summary of the billions of bits that the computer must sort through each second. The "illusion" generated by the conscious mind is comparable.

Most of us are completely unaware that we are experiencing most of our lives on something like a video delay. It's such a short time—often only a third to half a second—that we factor it into our "normal" response time and pay no attention. It's the time it takes to process our perceptions through our nervous system and come up with some idea of what is going on.

"Identify a dog or a tree or an apple pie"

We take in millions of bits of information *per second* through our senses, but only a couple dozen bits actually make it to our conscious minds. It's about a million to one reduction. By the time I can consciously identify a dog or a tree or an apple pie, my nervous system has discarded millions of bits of information and is gearing up for the next onslaught. The moment is gone by the time I can identify it.

The Greek philosopher Heraclitus famously said, "You could not step twice into the same river; for other waters are ever flowing on to you." By the time I am aware of the water molecules that bathe my feet, those particles are well downstream. It's the same with any other experience.

It takes time to process the electrical impulses of our nervous system and summarize the millions of bits of information into a cogent thought consisting of the couple dozen bits that our conscious minds can handle each second. It's tantamount to using Twitter to describe exactly what each instrument in an orchestra is playing moment by moment. By the time you type in "oboe," Beethoven's *Eroica Symphony* has moved on several bars and you haven't even considered the piccolo and cello. Our minds just don't have the RAM to process the fullness of What-is. Nor do all the computers in the world daisy-chained together.

Physicist and philosopher Herman Weyl writes:

Only to the gaze of my consciousness, crawling along the life-line of my body, does a section of the world come to life as a fleeting image in space which continually changes in time.

It's not easy to notice the lag time of the nervous system since most of our fellow humans are doing the same thing: having experiences and conducting their own ongoing internal narrative. Ordinary human interactions allow for this slow churn.

However, some activities—martial arts, sports, emergencies—may pull us out of our daze by demanding that we deal with what is going on Now! When sparring, or facing a 120 mph serve, or skidding on black ice…that half-second can be an eternity. I stopped playing baseball long before I figured out how to hit a fastball. I would still be puzzling out what to do as the strike was called. Superior athletes know they can't overthink an action and still be effective. They familiarize themselves with probable situations so their choices are better known and easier to make. They don't equivocate. They just DO.

We often find ourselves exhilarated by our brushes with immediacy. For many it is the only time they feel they aren't stuck in their head. This is part of the attraction of extreme sports or car racing. "So much is happening so fast, and I can't really consider all the implications right now because if I do, something really bad will likely happen. But isn't this FUN!"

These are events when we abruptly awaken from the It-trance. The curtain parts for a moment and we see things as they really are... before the story kicks in and we say "this is not that." It may be a time of crisis or exquisite beauty, and we are awe-struck. Words fail us. The birth of a child. An exquisite dance. A first kiss. Our ongoing narrative is interrupted by an ineffable clarity...for a moment...or two.

Then it starts up again: What was that? Is it like something I already know? Is it new? Is it dangerous? How could I describe it to my friends? Can I get it back? The words return as we try to find a box big enough to encapsulate whatever part of the event we remember taking in. The story returns us to the World of It.

There is a qualitative difference between the actual event and the internal narrative we use to explain it. They correspond like a birthday cake and a recipe in a book. When we forget this seemingly obvious distinction—and we will—we "con-fuse" (fuse together) the appearance of something with what it actually is. We re-enter the It-trance.

As long as we remember that the story is not really What-is, but only how it appears to us from a particular perspective, we can safely and joyfully navigate the It-world.

Every experience is a paradox in that it means to be absolute, and yet is relative; in that it somehow always goes beyond itself and yet never escapes itself.

T.S. Eliot

Chapter 10

Appearances

Those who experience do not participate in the world. For the experience is "in them" and not between them and the world. The world does not participate in experience. It allows itself to be experienced, but it is not concerned, for it contributes nothing, and nothing happens to it.

Martin Buber

Experience is the subject of the branch of philosophy called *phenomenology:* the study of phenomena (Latin, from Greek *phainómenon* "thing appearing to view"). Phenomena are the way things appear to us, and all experience is based on appearances.

Driving through the desert you see the horizon line so clearly that you could draw it with a crayon. But that horizon exists for you only as an idea based on your relationship to it in the moment. You can drive forever and never arrive at the horizon.

But that doesn't make it less real.

That is what reality is: how What-is appears to us. And that reality gets more substantial if others agree with your interpretation of how things appear. We can only experience things as they seem to be, not as they are. When others agree with us, we feel more certain about our perceptions.

We go through events and label our impressions of the surfaces of things, tell ourselves a story about them, and then fit that story in with other stories about other phenomena. That is, we run an event through our nervous system to sort it out and then file that away for future reference. We make inferences. When we bring our story to mind again, we are interacting with the memory, not the thing itself.

Experience begins with an awareness of the event and includes our perceptions, thoughts, and feelings about it. The event must capture some of our attention to qualify. The body-mind picks up signals all the time, but only a few actually come to our attention.

In *Landscapes of the Mind,* LeShan writes, "Each species has a sensory array that gives it a specific world picture. This is the world picture that makes it most likely that the species will survive."

Dogs hear sounds and smell things that are beyond human range. We two-leggers may be present when a dog whistle blows, but the sound isn't happening for us. The frequency is too high. And while you and I see the red of the fire engine, Fido only has color receptors for yellow and greenish-blue.

Recognizing the limitations of experience grants us the freedom to be just what we are. We are not omniscient creatures, capable of knowing everything. Nor are we benighted and stumbling in a cruel, capricious chaos. We can perceive some things and figure out others. And we can make maps. And maps of maps.

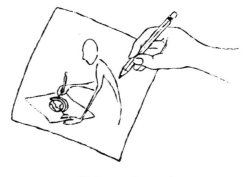

"Maps of maps"

I will never see electrons spinning around the nucleus of an atom. I'm okay with that. And atoms ain't what they used to be.

The theory told now about atoms is very different from the one I learned in high school chemistry. Forget those three-dimensional models showing electrons, neutrons, and protons. Not even close.

An actual atom is almost entirely empty space. If the space were removed from the atoms that make up the Empire State Building, the "stuff" that remained would be the size of a grain of rice.

How do I know this? It is a story shared by a scientist (Brian Greene) about the current paradigm, told in a way I could imagine. I'm sure the reality that he and his science buddies share is much more complex than that. They speak a mathematical language that is far beyond my ken.

Which is "true?" Both. And neither. They give some insight into something that can never be known completely. Even my old high school model is "true" in a way. And each of these is different from the theory postulated by the Greek philosopher Democritus (460–370 B.C.), who saw atoms as indivisible spheres that linked via mechanical means.

These "useful fictions" are all based on inferences based on other inferences, organized into a package that we find useful in some way. That process is the warp and woof of the It-world. We repeat it each time we experience.

Our perceptions are colored by maps of prior experiences and are woven into a story that tries to make sense of what is happening. Even "inner experiences" (dreams, emotions, thoughts, for example) are known by their appearances and become part of that complex worldview.

We label external objects (ostrich, ebb tide, pinot noir) and internal ones (sadness, hunger, bliss) so we can tell our story. We objectify (make into an object) whatever we label. Our words can only capture a small part of what is actually happening, but we piece different descriptions together and come up with ideas about it. As imperfect as our maps are, they provide the foundation for further discovery.

Levels of Abstraction

Korzybski emphasized that any object that we experience is in a state of change, even when that change is not apparent. He wrote, "It must be stated that 'identity,' [his single quotes denoting common misunderstanding] defined as 'absolute sameness,' necessitates 'absolute sameness' in 'all' aspects, never to be found in this world, nor in our heads. Anything with which we deal on the objective levels represents a process."

For instance, it is a "useful fiction" that my body-mind is the same one that started this sentence. But even in that brief time huge changes have occurred. In each of the tens of trillions of cells that constitute my physical body, there are countless physicochemical processes each second. Millions of cells have also been shed and replaced by entirely different cells. Anything that I can label is changing.

Whatever is actually unchanging about me is not an It.

Our minds try to freeze moments through abstraction. We disconnect from the incessant whirl of events long enough to get some perspective.

Similarities appear only as a result of the action of our nervous system, which does not register absolute differences. Therefore, we register similarities, which evaporate when our means of investigation become more subtle. Similarities are read into nature by our nervous system.

Korzybski

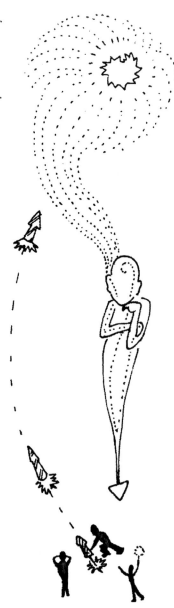

Whenever I "think about" something, those abstractions are compared to other abstractions I have made. My mind reviews my previous thoughts, intuitions, impressions, inferences, and conclusions. It dutifully tries to fit all the new information I am taking in into the story I have been working on for decades ("My Life"), but only the tiniest fragment actually gets my conscious attention. Even less is deemed important enough to commit to memory.

And each level of abstraction takes us further from the actual event that is occurring Now.

The process begins with an event: for example, the explosion of a firecracker. The air vibrates, which causes more vibrations in the adjacent space and continues until they reach my body-mind, which also then resonates with them. Then comes my perception of that sound, which comes some time *after* the event (sound travels

"Perceiving the sounds of fireworks"

approximately 1129 feet per second at sea level at 70 degrees F) and includes only a small part of possible information about the event. The sound is loud and unusual enough to get the attention of my conscious mind, which then begins the process of figuring out what I just heard.

My nervous system compares my perceptions with the usual suspects from my past and comes up with a description of the event. I make some inferences based on this description, like "That was a loud noise, but not dangerous to me," and "I bet the McGillicutty kids are celebrating the Fourth of July a little early." Then I may make inferences about my inferences and inferences about those inferences... .

Each inference potentially becomes part of my reality. If any of those inferences seems interesting or important enough, it is committed to memory. The event, what I now call "a firecracker," is part of What-is. My perceptions and inferences about the event—after the event—are my reality and the story I tell about the event.

This process became clearer to me in recent years as I began noticing a delay between hearing what someone said and actually understanding what was meant. Some aural frequencies have been sacrificed to the gods of rock'n'roll, and there is a second or two of inferring what those sounds are actually saying.

If someone speaks with a thick or unfamiliar accent, the same process is required to sort out what is being said. There is a delay—sometimes a second or two—between the hearing and the understanding of those words.

There is a time lag with any perception, including vision, as your nervous system sorts out what just happened.

Communication depends on inferences made by the receiver, and the inferences then become the objects of our experience. Attention moves from the sounds, to what was intended by those sounds, to what we think about what we thought was actually said. The same process occurs with each of our senses.

It is these levels of objectification (abstraction) that give meaning to an event. They are the building blocks of knowledge. They are also the source of the prevailing Trance of Objectivity that pervades the It-world. Each level of abstraction takes us deeper into the confusion of appearances until objects are all there is. And that includes you and me and everyone we know.

Knowledge depends on abstraction, and never before have we been able to store and share so much knowledge. This era has been dubbed the Age of Information. We are bombarded with abstraction each time we use a book, computer, or television. Small children have their own smart phones. Teenagers text or tweet a friend sitting across a table. You can stuff a library into a Kindle or iPad, and are but a few mouse clicks removed from an incomprehensibly vast Web of electronic abstraction.

It is commonplace now to construct an online identity and interact with other virtual identities (all abstractions) in abstracted online environments. An I.D. number or a barcode exists for everything, in order for it to be easily tracked by ubiquitous computers.

There is nothing inherently bad about any of this. It presents opportunities beyond the dreams of our ancestors, as well as the promise of much more. We can travel across continents in hours and videoconference with someone half a world away. These applications of technology are the expression of who we are and what we consider important.

We can become lost in our abstraction, however, taking us deeper into the trance. The objects we think we see aren't even the objects themselves. Psychologist Erich Fromm wrote, "The tree we ordinarily see has no individuality…it is only the representative of an abstraction." We can't see the trees or the forest, but rather an idea of both.

But that doesn't make them any less real.

Before abstraction everything is one, but one like chaos; after abstraction everything is united again, but this union is a free binding of autonomous, self-determined beings.

Novalis, poet and philosopher

Chapter 11
People as Objects

Life's but a walking shadow, a poor player
That struts and frets his hour upon the stage
And then is heard no more. It is a tale
Told by an idiot, full of sound and fury,
Signifying nothing.

Macbeth, Act 5, Scene 5

In the It-world, people are objects too.

A living, breathing, feeling person is replaced in our minds by a concept, a representation. This is what we do with anything we think about. But when the It-trance kicks in, we forget that the mind-object is just that...an object. Then we get caught up experiencing an idea, not the actual person. We may see "a poor player that struts and frets his hour upon the stage" or a bodhisattva. Both are abstractions of What-is.

One common example of getting lost in the It-trance is the animated argument we have in our own mind with someone who isn't there. We can get pretty worked up about how "unreasonable" our debate partner is being, and feel all the emotional and physical effects of contentiousness. People make some crazy choices based on a controversy with a mind-object of their own fabrication. If the trance is deep enough, it can even lead to paranoia or violent fury.

The It-trance occludes authentic moments of genuine relation. It leaves stick-figure sketches as reminders of what we think might happen.

Even the liveliest of us gets flattened by Wile E. Coyote's steamroller into a two-dimensional pancake.

Objectification, of course, is as important as it is inevitable. When we talk or think about people, they must be abstracted. We can't include all the information, just the highlights. It's easier to think of a rock or a toaster as an object than it is Grandma or little Susie, but anytime we label a person, we substitute a symbol for the actual person.

Although we can—and must—objectify people in order to think about them, a sane person is aware that *ideas about* people are not the same thing as who and what they really are. However, in the It-trance we forget that. The objectified person becomes the label. ("The Great Emancipator," "Vlad the Impaler," "The Buddha.")

All labels are brief expressions of our experience. We cannot think in any detailed way without them. And just as any experience of a hairbrush or a hot shower or a pizza must be incomplete, so must any experience of another person…no matter how intimate.

Please remember, we are defining "experience" as *the direct observation of or participation in events as a basis of knowledge.* Experience is not just "something that happens." It also requires that some sentient being be aware that some event is happening.

Experience of persons also happens in the past. All that is remembered are the surface impressions: our ideas about them. Those get labeled and sorted in all the ways we can think about human beings.

You and I may have just had the most wonderful time together, but whenever either of us thinks about the other later, it will be as an It. We can certainly use our fond memories of each other to summon up warm, fuzzy feelings, but these memories are mind-objects too. And with them come our thoughts and emotions about them, and our thoughts and emotions about those thoughts and emotions.

For example: "Joe has such a great sense of humor. He's an excellent listener too." Here I'm telling my story about Joe, and I'm already comparing him to other people in my mind. (His humor is "great." His listening skills are "excellent.")

I make inferences as part of my experience, and those inferences are being updated and refreshed every time I bring my attention to them. As with any experience, my thoughts about what just happened feed back into my existing database, and I bring that to the next moment. ("You know, what I was just thinking about Joe...that's really true. He is a funny guy.") Inferences are made about inferences.

Or I may intuit from the way the boss greets me that she's in a bad mood today and this is not the time to ask for a raise. Maybe I was just joking around with a co-worker moments ago, but quickly downshift into "appropriate office behavior" to relate better to a scowling superior.

My inferences (based on surface impressions) color my experience of her and also affect her perceptions of me. Before we even start our little minuet of office etiquette, we have already objectified each other as "boss" and "employee," and that establishes the parameters of our exchange. Each of those roles comes with expectations and limits.

When we experience a person, we consider their qualities or attributes: how they appear to us. Tall, short, clever, dull, beautiful, or ugly—there are lots of ways to describe how people are perceived. We label the *dramatis personae* in our story to explain and remember what roles they play. It also reminds us of the parts that we play in those stories.

Dad and Mom let us know early on how we should behave toward them in their role as parents. Affection, respect, loyalty, obedience. From them we get a foundation in civilized human interaction. Teacher, doctor, boss, police officer, playmate—there is an etiquette, tacit or expressed, that circumscribes what are appropriate actions and attitudes in our dealings with each of them.

A lot of our attention goes to learning the functions that we and others perform. We assume personas that are appropriate to those functions. They differ from who we are as people, but in the It-trance that distinction is lost. We become the characters that we play in our functions. Many of us never get past our roles as children or parents and learn to relate to each other in any other way.

People Maps

We categorize a person in many ways, such as race, religion, nationality, sex, profession, social class, attractiveness, political beliefs, or sports team affiliation. We abstract some of the qualities of a unique individual to create an object that we can then compare and contrast with other objects of abstraction. Noticing differences and similarities enables us to construct a story: "Mommy is a doctor. She has brown hair. Daddy is an Egyptologist. He has a mustache."

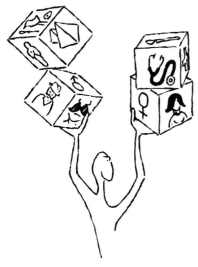

"Constructing a story about mom and dad"

Even when our descriptions are accurate, they can never be complete. The story is never a full substitute for the person being represented, but it may be a useful map if it describes the territory with some accuracy.

Does it help us to actually understand this person better? Does it open a window to who and what they really are? Is the story consistent with what is known or observable? Should the map be revised to reflect changes? Does our narrative bring us closer to What-is?

First impressions are important, because we base our initial map of people on how their current behavior fits with our previous inferences. Those impressions influence all subsequent interactions, accurately or not. When our previous inferences are sufficiently intractable, it's called a prejudice: the mind is already made up. Human history is filled with stories of people willing to kill and die for their prejudices.

Some maps hang around long after they've been shown to be invalid. For instance, if I'm asked, "What is the moon made of?" the first answer I think of is, "Green cheese." Why? Because it's something I heard as a child and it stuck. It doesn't matter that it's nonsense. It has sentimental value.

All over the world people cling to beliefs that have no more substance than that. When those beliefs are superimposed over What-is, the maps can be pretty unreliable. When they are confused with the territory, then things can get really ugly. Racial intolerance, sexual bias, religious hatred, and homophobia are but a few examples of how humans can be unfairly objectified by other humans. Faulty maps based on insufficient and incorrect ideas twist and distort the actual human being into an object to be treated with fear, scorn, and even violence.

As we develop, we must work our way through the many maps we encounter from our families, friends, tribes, cultures, and religions. Some of the prejudices we learn are helpful to surviving childhood ("Don't get into a car with a stranger.") But the lessons may also be the unprocessed bile of a culture or a subgroup.

We can be tranced by our culture, religion, education, and government to believe a lot of really crazy stuff. It may take a lifetime to find which maps work best for you.

Whenever two people meet, there are really six people present. There is each man as he sees himself, each man as the other person sees him, and each man as he really is.

William James

Chapter 12

Numbers Do Lie...
That's Their Job

As far as the laws of mathematics refer to reality, they are not certain; and as far as they are certain, they do not refer to reality.

Albert Einstein

Modern science draws much of its validity from its ability to express the world in a mathematical language. There is a beauty and clarity to mathematics that only the high priests trained in that lexicon can appreciate. The It-world is about experience and utilization, and mathematics tells the tale in a precise and valuable way.

The hard sciences (physics, chemistry, geology) have had great success applying their mathematical models to all the physical stuff in the world. The soft sciences like psychology, sociology, and economics use statistical models to gain insight into human behavior. Doing so requires describing people and their actions and qualities in mathematical symbols. These can be recognized as meaningful by computers that think in terms of ones and zeroes. Such models are helpful in estimating things like expected voter turnout in a non-presidential election, the life expectancy of a thirty-year old non-smoking female in Tuscaloosa, or the marketability of a new deodorant.

While useful in predicting certain patterns in human behavior, there is an underlying flaw in mathematical representation that is so obvious that it is often ignored. It's the same one that pervades non-numerical abstractions: confusing the map with the territory.

We often hear that numbers don't lie. This statement is somewhat accurate...but in only one place: the world of the mind. That is, numbers are unfailingly dependable where the rules are defined as mental constructs. But numbers are ideas—useful fictions—and are as fallible as any other idea when asked to do actual work.

Mathematics can be a powerful tool when used to represent some part of What-is, but their capacity to truthfully answer a question is limited by our ability to ask the right question. The question must be answerable as a number.

Korzybski loved mathematics, but also knew its place, "Only and exclusively in mathematics does deduction, if correct, work absolutely, for no particulars are left out which may later be discovered and force us to modify our deductions.... . We build for ourselves a fictitious and over-simplified verbal world."

"Two plus two equals four" is often used to punctuate a statement deemed so obviously logical that it couldn't possibly be argued. That's because that simple equation seems a certainty. Yet, when is it actually true?

Let's say we have two children, Samantha and Pete. Along comes two more, Jill and Willard. My arithmetic tells me we now have four children. And in an abstract sense we do. (The *idea* of two objects plus the *idea* of two more similar objects can now be identified as the *idea* of four objects with something in common.)

But most parents don't consider their actual offspring as interchangeable with other children. Each is unique. "One child" cannot actually equal one child, even when we are talking about the "same" child. Why? We can no more replace Samantha with Pete than we can substitute accurately this Pete for the "Pete that used to be."

A can never "equal" *A*, except as an abstraction where all differences are ignored. Pete does not equal any other Pete, even the Pete from thirty seconds ago. (If only because millions of Pete's cells have come and gone in that short time.) But sometimes it is useful to think that it does.

One apple does *not* equal one apple, but I happily overlook that fact when purchasing a dozen apples. The farmer doesn't care to discuss non-Aristotelian logic when people are lined up to buy produce from him. He wants to sell as many of these objects as he can and get home before dark. It is useful to both of us to overlook the discrepancies that exist between apples and to think mathematically.

It is a "useful fiction."

Death and Numbers

There are three types of lies: lies, damn lies, and statistics.

Benjamin Disraeli

Stalin said, "One death is a tragedy. One million deaths is a statistic." He cruelly and methodically orchestrated the deaths of tens of millions of his own countrymen. They weren't people to him, merely numbers.

Humans are incapable of imagining that much suffering. But if we convert it to a statistic, we can tell the story in numbers without experiencing the soul-crushing monstrosity of that event. It becomes an idea that we can hold in the mind, and even compare with the barbarities of other twentieth-century sociopaths (Hitler, Mao, Pol Pot—to name a few).

As a New Yorker, the events of September 11, 2001 are still vivid in my mind. The smoke. The smells. The darkness. The chaos. Yet, I don't claim to have more than a superficial understanding of what happened. No one can. The official version tells us that 2,977 victims died that day. More died later.

Converting the horror into a number story gives us enough distance to move forward. A big hole is paved over.

Then I think of the tens of thousands of Iraqi innocents felled by American bombs, and it's even harder to imagine. The number saves me. I can't imagine ONE child blown up by an explosion partially subsidized by my taxes, much less thousands. But statistics spare us the details.

The mind can soften those events further by comparing them to the tens of thousands of people in the U.S. killed each year by themselves and others using guns or automobiles. They are "fatalities," and a fatality is not a person. It is a mind-object that can be counted.

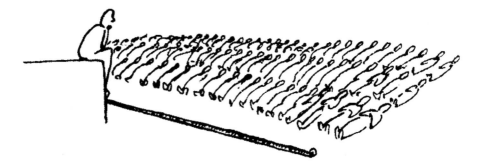

Suffering cannot be measured, but corpses can.

Creating a story is that most human of abilities. Forgetting it is a story is that most human of frailties.

No truly human characteristics can be described in any world picture that has quantitative aspects. Those observables which make us uniquely human, including compassion, love, loyalty, courage.... None of these can be measured quantitatively.

Lawrence LeShan

Chapter 13
The Object Is Me

Actually, I...this may sound a little West Texan to you, but I like it. When I'm talking about...when I'm talking about myself, and when he's talking about myself, all of us are talking about me.

George W. Bush

Just as we must objectify others to make sense of the parts they play in our narrative, we must also do so to our own selves. And ME seems to pop up a lot in our stories.

We are more than our body, mind, experience, energy, history, heritage, hopes and dreams, beliefs, nationality, race...anything we can say about ourselves. We are more than the sum of our parts. Each quality adds substance to how we perceive ourselves and how others see us, but describes surfaces only. The depth of who you are defies any description. Yet surface and depth both contribute to our identity.

We are assembling our sense of self moment by moment. It is fluid and ever changing. We are each the protagonist of our own movie, which is constantly revised and edited. Each new experience, and our response to it, shapes us—adding to the known and opening to the unknown. Our minds continually update what we think about ourselves, in order to function in a rapidly changing world. Each challenge we face presents an opportunity to get a clearer sense of who we are.

We may think the past is fixed, but new information and perspectives come to light and cast even our bedrock assumptions and beliefs into doubt. The "past" does not exist as an entity. It is a story cobbled together from remembered bits and inferences about inferences. Winston Churchill joked, "History will be kind to me, for I intend to write it."

As much as we strive for truth, our narratives are riddled with inaccuracies, speculations, prejudices, gross exaggerations, and outright fabrications. And no matter how well we think we remember what came before, those events no longer exist. All we have are our inferences about them. And we all remember things a little differently.

There is a memorable exchange in a song in the movie *Gigi* between Honoré and Mamita:

H: We met at nine M: We met at eight
H: I was on time M: No, you were late
H: Ah, yes, I remember it well
H: We dined with friends M: We dined alone
H: A tenor sang M: A baritone
H: Ah, yes, I remember it well

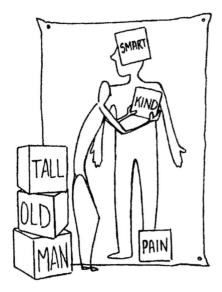

"Our narratives are the maps of who and what we think we are"

As inaccurate as they must be, our narratives are the maps of who and what we think we are. They chronicle our journey from the distant past to the present moment and remind us of what we consider to be important. We seek security in an uncertain world and hold back the chaos with our words. Even untrue or unkind words offer us comfort if the pain they hide is much worse.

Experience provides us with an externally derived identity. It is externally derived in that it is based on observing the effects of our interactions with the world. We weave that information into what we already know and try to come up with a coherent story. This provides context and continuity in our lives, and some version of it is necessary to function in the world. Those who have lost their story—like amnesiacs and Alzheimer's sufferers—are rudderless in choppy seas.

In the It-world, we sense and objectify the elements of our experience, including ourselves. We observe our own interactions with the stuff of life, analyze them, make corrections, and then fit that into our ideas about how the world works and what our role is in it.

Life challenges us to explore the range of our abilities and limitations. We record our experiences for future reference. The motivation for constructing these tales is to continue existing for a bit longer. The narratives clue us in on conditions and behaviors that help or hurt us.

My experience tells me that if I want to fly, I will need a mechanical device—like an airplane or helicopter—to get my otherwise earthbound body airborne. It is a limitation I cheerfully accept in my role as a bipedal hominid, and it is part of my story.

That doesn't stop me from flying in my dreams though.

Ego

What we call *ego* is an objectification of the self.

The ego is who and what I consider myself to be. It is the character I play in the story I generate. That changes with each passing moment, and self-image changes with it.

It is the experience of my self…as an object. And, as with any object, the Me that appears to view is not, and cannot be, the whole package. Any image of self is distorted—like the sound of your own voice. (I'm still surprised sometimes when I hear a recording of me talking or singing.) Alan Watts said, "Trying to define yourself is like trying to bite your own teeth."

You can consider a few of your qualities at any moment, but the You that is aware of being aware is unknowable. The sum total of all your qualities does not begin to approach the miracle that is You. You are not your hair, name, mind, heart, profession, or reputation. Anything you can think about is not you.

Ego often has a bad connotation in popular culture. People associate the term with selfishness and narcissism. Many spiritual teachers tell us that the ego must be annihilated to attain "enlightenment." Certainly, an obsession with how one appears to self and others can distract from What-is, but ego serves an important function in our lives. Annihilation might be an inappropriate sentence for the crime of identifying who and what you appear to be.

"*Non-objective awareness cannot be maintained while functioning as a human*"

Non-objective awareness is expansive and liberating, but it cannot be maintained while functioning as a human. Anyone who has some idea of who they are and what they are doing has an ego. Lao-tse, Buddha, and Jesus all did. It is a sign of mental dysfunction if you don't.

Far from being an impediment to spiritual awakening, the ego provides each of us with a unique perspective from which we can engage life.

Nobelist Max Plank, originator of quantum theory wrote:

The fact is that there is a point, one single point in the immeasurable world of mind and matter, where science and therefore every causal method of research is inapplicable, not only on practical grounds but also on logical grounds, and will always remain inapplicable. This point is the individual ego. It is a small point in the universal realm of being, but, in itself, it is a whole world, embracing our emotional life, our will, and our thought. The realm of the ego is, at once, the source of our deepest suffering and, at the same time, of our highest happiness.

Das Ich und Das Es

Sigmund Freud is the person usually credited with popularizing the term ego. However, he actually used *das Ich* (German for "the I"). "Ego" appeared later when Freud was translated to English by James Strachey, who used a Latin pronoun rather than the English "I." (The Latin *ego* is sometimes translated as "I myself" for emphasis.)

Freud also used *das Es* ("the It"), which was similarly given the Latin treatment and morphed into "the Id." (One could say that *Das Ich* uses reason and judgment to make sense of *Das Es*.) The I. The It. The Ego. The Id.

As far as we know, infants have no ego. It is thought that their nervous systems have not yet reached the stage where such a distinction is possible. Their consciousness is undifferentiated—there is no distinction between *Das Ich* and *Das Es,* The I and The It. Our nervous systems register sensations and execute genetically pre-programmed survival functions, but there is no I or You or It yet.

We bump against the solid things of the world until a primitive map begins to appear in our minds. At some point we are able to stick a pin in the map to mark the point we are able to distinguish as "me." Then comes the awareness of "not-me," and that opens up our worlds to many exciting possibilities.

Until we learn to distinguish *Das Ich* from *Das Es*, we are part of the events we encounter in our young lives with no understanding of what is going on. We eat and poop and pee and react to external stimuli, but are not yet able to construct a story. Not yet. We ARE the pain of the diaper rash or colic. We notice things and react to them before our nervous systems mature enough to distinguish differences and similarities.

But one day the light goes on and the fusion of consciousness is split by a new awareness that mommy is somehow different from me. From that point, our minds divide and differentiate like the zygote we once were. From this yang and yin we develop our own experience of the It-world. Other humans teach us to name and map these phenomena until we work out our own systems.

We are still bumping into things many years later and forming our concept of who and/or what we are with each bump. We are challenged to revise our place in the world in ways large and small, and sometimes have to update our self-image abruptly.

A growing child is surprised by how her old haunts seem so small now. A man is shocked when his old jeans won't fit him. A woman looks in a mirror and says, "I have become my mother!"

Each new skill learned, ability lost, heart broken, toe stubbed, accolade received, or criticism suffered has some effect on our sense of identity.

You can't play any game in life without some sense of self. Ego is the vehicle through which we relate to others. It becomes distorted when our image of who and what we are veers too far from the evidence that greets our senses. Or when we become too attached to a particular self-image and try to use it in the wrong situations.

For example, the high point of Marsha's life was being voted Homecoming Queen thirty years ago, but her inability to move on locks her into an inappropriate identity now that she's obese and living on welfare. Edgar suffered humiliation and abuse often in his childhood and can't shed his poor self-image to ask for a much-deserved raise at work. Susan controls her business with an iron hand and extends the same dominating personality in her non-work relationships.

Marsha, Edgar, and Susan are all stuck in a fixed idea of who and what they are and are unable or unwilling to adjust to new and different situations. A healthy ego is constantly adapting to changes in circumstances, while maintaining a core identity that makes it recognizable and dependable to others.

But even the healthiest ego is not really "who we are."

Ego is a mind object, useful and even necessary. But like any object, it belongs to the realm of experience and is a surface impression only. You are not your name, your body, your job, your past, your experiences, or your thoughts. Anything you experience is already gone. All you have of it are the memories. The story.

Whatever you say the object is, well, it is not.

Alfred Korzybski

Chapter 14
Wholeness

Being alive is to achieve the long range coordination of astronomical numbers of submicroscopic, molecular reactions over macroscopic distances; it is to be able to summon energy at will and to engage in extremely rapid and efficient energy transduction.

Mae Wan Ho, geneticist

Okay, so how do we make the jump from treating ourselves and others as conceptual objects, and start really connecting with each other?

How do we find You in a World of It?

It is hard to let go of the It-mind when it is what ties your whole story together. Our brief flirtations with I-You often send us scurrying back to the more familiar terrain of the It-world.

So we have to take in an important step before we get back to Finding You.

The missing step is Wholeness. That is, we encounter another with our whole being. Most of us aren't able to do that very often. But sometimes it just happens.

We have all had experiences—however fleeting—when it all just came together. We were "in the Zone," "in Flow," "inspired." Maybe it was something thrilling like playing an intricate guitar solo, or making an impossible grab off third base and nailing the runner with a blind throw to first, or transfixing the audience with a spellbinding oration. Or maybe it was something as prosaic as deftly avoiding an accident on a busy freeway, or calming a roomful of children with a smile and a few words.

During these moments we are not self-conscious. Things just happen the way they should…without a struggle, without second-guessing, without fear. They just flow. We may not even notice at the time. After all, we successfully achieved our objective and moved on to the next challenge. Maybe later, though, the improbability of the event comes to mind and we feel again the satisfaction of our moment of effortless competence.

One prominent characteristic of Wholeness is that the mind clears. It doesn't shut down into a state of unawareness or fill up with daydreams. It suspends its internal dialogue of contrast and compare and somehow "knows" what to do.

"Carving ourselves into little pieces"

We have momentary flashes of non-objective awareness in those moments.

Those moments in Wholeness feel great when we notice them. Then we get right back to carving ourselves into little pieces. That's what the It-mind does so well. It separates us out through objectification.

So, how do you get past that to feel whole whenever you want?

You might be surprised to know that it is not only possible but surprisingly simple. It's a technique I discovered in my martial arts training and have been using for a long time. If you and I were to meet on the street, well, I would take you through a short demonstration. You would feel it…in your body-mind. It would take just a few minutes.

But this is a book, and I'm trying to explain this in words. If a picture is worth a thousand words, then a demonstration is worth ten thousand. If you've never been kissed by a person that you find attractive, words are no substitute. You need that person to plant one on you. You can talk about it later.

Wholeness is even trickier. There are no fireworks, no brass band, no angel choir. It's subtle, but life-changing. Wholeness is essential to breaking free of the It-trance. For those of us that spend our day entranced by objectivity, the concept of personal Wholeness is a distant ideal. Our minds are rarely in a state of peaceful unity.

The It-mind, even at its most benign, creates an artificial separation from ourselves. But more often, that self-separation leads to a spiral of self-critique and attack that furthers the fragmentation and distance from our Wholeness.

We edit, criticize, berate, and second-guess ourselves regularly. Internal monologue is filled with blame, shame, and regret. Negative emotions and critical thoughts shatter the Wholeness. There is a deep chasm between the self that is being criticized and the self that is doing the criticizing. And that feeds further negativity/fragmentation.

Engaging another as You must be done with your whole being. In Wholeness we resonate with What-is, temporarily freed from our habitual objectification. The It-mind distrusts extended stays in non-objective awareness. It prefers the order and structure of a well-crafted narrative, even when it's a story that makes you miserable.

We stand outside ourselves whenever we experience ourselves as objects. Self-esteem and self-rebuke both require abstraction. There is an unspecified distance between the "me" that is praised or minimized and the "I" that is doing the praising/minimizing. It's that way with any personal narrative, and it's the only way we can make sense of what is happening.

However, when we are inside the Wholeness, it is different. There is no self-consciousness. There is just Now.

Over two thousand years ago, Zhuangzi (Chuang-tsu), wrote:

When a drunken man falls from a carriage, though the carriage may be going very fast, he won't be killed. He has bones and joints the same as other men, and yet he is not injured as they would be, because his spirit is whole. He didn't know he was riding, and he doesn't know he has fallen out. Life and death, alarm and terror do not enter his breast, and so he can bang against things without fear of injury. If he can keep himself whole like this by means of wine, how much more can he keep himself whole by means of Dao.

Like Zhuangzi's drunkard, in Wholeness we are not concerned with self as an object. When we resonate with Dao (What-is), we don't think about it…we just do. And we DO at a higher level of effectiveness than with a divided mind.

Martial artists learn to unify body and mind to perform highly improbable feats, like smashing cement blocks with their fists or making daring leaps. Actors lose their self-consciousness and immerse themselves in their roles. A painter's inner vision explodes on the canvas. A meditator enters a state of "pure consciousness"—full of awareness, but unfocused on any *thing*.

More mundane experiences of this state are found often in our daily lives. In fact, we are constantly moving in and out of them. Most are ignored since our nervous system rarely registers eventless moments, favoring instead moments of action or conflict. This state is so commonplace that most instances of it are filtered out by our ever-vigilant nervous systems. Our nervous systems are usually preoccupied with recognizing, anticipating, and resolving dangers—past, present, and future—real or imagined in our lives.

Yet these moments of clear-minded action abound in our normality. They are so predictable—effortlessly driving a car, typing an email, playing a video game—that we would be embarrassed to consider them in the same light as an Olympic record javelin throw, a yogi passing a needle through his flesh, or an impassioned speech touching the hearts and minds of millions.

They all have something in common: complex activities done so well that they do not require self-conscious thought. We take them for granted and quickly move on to thoughts about other challenges. We hardly notice the moments of effortless competence.

So what is the big deal? We all have skills that come so easily to us that we can casually do something that would mystify someone somewhere. A woodworker thinks little of operating a bandsaw, but an unskilled person might be terrified of losing a thumb. A child easily operates a computer that would stymie his parents.

Magicians practice their card tricks until the physical action requires so little attention that they can focus on snappy patter to entertain and distract their audience. And we are baffled by how the queen of hearts ended up under the vase. Piece of cake to their fellow prestidigitators, but seemingly impossible to those not clued in.

So if this state is so commonplace why even mention it?

Because one of the most important treasures imaginable is hidden in plain view. Wholeness is obscured by the all the activities that it spawns. Our minds quickly reach for the next challenge and fail to nurse this precious ember into a bright flame.

Something very special happens in a state of Wholeness. It is alchemical. Body, mind, and spirit integrate.

"Body, mind, and spirit integrate"

In the next chapter we find out how to get there…fast.

The extent of your consciousness is limited only by your ability to love and embrace with your love the space around you, and all it contains.

Napoleon Bonaparte

Chapter 15

Coherence

The idea of eternity lives in all of us. We thirst to live in a belief which raises our small personality to a higher coherence—a coherence which is human and yet superhuman, absolute and yet steadily growing and developing, ideal and yet real.

Christian Louis Lange, historian

There is a simple technique I developed in my martial arts training that helps to generate body-mind-spirit unity in a dramatic way. I noticed that exceptional performers of all types—martial artists, athletes, dancers, singers—would often reach with their hands to enhance their ability. I experimented for years and eventually found that pointing and reaching with the index finger dramatically and instantly increased my effective power.

Not just a little...A LOT!

95

I said it was a simple technique. That's why I find it easier to demonstrate than to talk about. I like people to feel it before the It-mind starts to come up with all the reasons why such a thing is not possible.

It's so improbable that some people dismiss it without even giving it a fair try. After all, they have pointed their index fingers for decades and never noticed anything special. Even when they see it demonstrated, there is often skepticism. It doesn't fit with what they already thought they knew. Their first impulse is to assume that a mistake has been made or that it is a trick.

I mentioned earlier that one of the advantages about internal martial arts and energy healing is that they slow things way down. You notice things that others miss.

Of course, this is true in other practices, too. I look at an X-ray and see nothing special, but a skilled doctor knows which dark spot is the problem area. An experienced conductor can hear a recording of a symphony and know that the third chair bassoon made a mistake. I can't.

But I do notice subtle things that are invisible to people who haven't put in the decades of study and practice that I have. And this is a big one.

Trial by Combat

I put this particular technique through some rigorous testing in martial arts tournaments. When I used it, I was David with his sling—able to defeat much larger, stronger, and younger opponents. With this technique I had the ability to integrate body, mind, and spirit…even under duress. Fast. (Don't be discouraged if you don't immediately. It requires fine-tuning.)

In competition, we encounter the same fears that we find anytime we take a risk— fear of

"Able to defeat much larger, stronger, younger opponents"

failure, fear of success, of ridicule, fear of disappointment, or of getting hurt. It's just you and your opponent in the ring with a lot of people watching. The clock is ticking. It all counts…at least to you.

Your opponent would like to win, too, and comes out with lots of puzzles for you to solve. When you're tense and nervous, it is harder to solve them. You revert to old patterns, get predictable…fall into traps.

There are many temptations to get hooked into fear-based response patterns. An ancient stress response encoded in our DNA shifts us into the reptile brain of "fight, flight, or freeze." Blood exits from the parts of your brain that correlate to higher centers of cognition. Thus, you forget all the cool stuff you've been working on and revert to more primitive responses.

In my training, I explored different ways to short-circuit the downward spiral of fear-based behavior. When things moved in the wrong direction, my practice partner and I would stop and reset, noting where the wheels came off the cart. But how to quickly get back to the calm, centered effectiveness that is the hallmark of t'ai chi ch'uan? How to return to Wholeness? The answer was so simple I passed it a thousand times without seeing it.

I found that when I pointed my index fingers, my fear and anxiousness disappeared. My body-mind immediately performed at a much higher level.

I didn't have to wait for Wholeness to find me; I summoned it: by pointing my index fingers and reaching with them.

It was too easy!

This is counter-intuitive, I must confess. When someone grabs or shoves you, your first response is to deal with that immediate threat, not "point your index fingers!" It flies in the face of decades of conditioning and just seems dumb. Your body-mind tries to veto this foolishness by tensing muscles and closing down awareness.

But it works when you learn to trust it. In my thirty-plus years of Chinese martial arts, I have learned that it's not enough just to be able to *find* Wholeness. It has to become your best friend.

You establish a comfortable baseline of coherence and take it with you everywhere. There are lots of ways to lose it, so expect that. Each time you restore Wholeness, it becomes easier to do so. The effect is cumulative. You inculcate it by going to the well again and again.

Accessing Coherence

The important thing is not that this technique makes you stronger, but how it does it. The implications go far beyond whether you can knock down a large attacker or lift something you couldn't otherwise. Your increased power is a by-product of something much more important: *coherence.*

Systems theorist Ervin Laszlo wrote, "A system of finely tuned parts is a coherent system. Coherence means that every part in the system responds to every other part, compensating for deviations and reinforcing functional actions and relations."

How often have we heard "The whole is greater than the sum of its parts?" It is an accepted truth that a team acting as a unit is more effective than the same group of individuals acting on their own. Coherence is the degree that parts work smoothly to form a whole.

When you point and reach with your index finger, you become more coherent, and your effective power increases instantly and dramatically. You feel stable and balanced. The mind is calm and clear. There is no fear. Time seems to slow and you see events unfold faster than your nervous system can ordinarily process. It becomes easier to resonate with What-is.

How to Do This Wrong

There are a million ways to do this wrong, and I keep finding new ones. The first thing to realize is that this is a new skill you are learning. You are doing something different with your existing equipment. Nobelist William Bragg said, "The important thing in science is not so much to obtain new facts as to discover new ways of thinking about them."

You may think, "I've pointed my finger a gazillion times. What could I possibly learn about such a simple action?"

That one assumption might be the biggest barrier. It takes you right back into the trance. That finger that you pointed a gazillion times...*it doesn't exist anymore!* That "finger" only exists *in your narrative,* your story. It is only an *idea* of a finger you once knew.

The one that I am talking about here is the one that you feel *before* you think about it. Just as the pizza I remember is not the same as the one I'm eating now, the finger that I reach with is not the one I remember from three seconds ago.

This is not just a metaphysical musing; it is the key to shifting out of the It-mind and instantly returning to resonance with the present moment.

And we know that anytime you think about something…well… it takes time to come up with a concise version that your conscious mind can deal with. How much time? Maybe a quarter to half a second, depending on the situation. That's not a lot in our normal day-to-day interactions, but in martial arts a quarter second can be an eternity.

In non-objective awareness, responses seem to take no time at all. That is probably not the case, but they do happen faster than the nervous system can track.

You can also see that if you do this with mental detachment—as though you are an objective observer of the process…well, that's not going to work either. You conceptualize the process, your body, your self…and you have already moved out of Wholeness and into the It-trance. You are no longer participant, but an observer.

So, for this technique to work you have to satisfy the conditions of the protocol, and the most fundamental one is that you shift out of experiential mode and actually participate without reserve. There is time for skepticism later, after you actually *do* it. Korzybski said, "There are two ways to slide easily through life; to believe everything or to doubt everything. Both ways save us from thinking."

I showed this technique to a famous scientist in the field of consciousness research. It didn't go so well. He felt so threatened by this anomaly that he had to "disprove" it immediately. He grabbed another scientist and they concocted a "double-blind test" on each other to show

how it was not possible. He felt very self-satisfied and was bragging about it to some pretty girls at a party later.

He completely missed the point of the exercise, of course. His skepticism ensured failure because he wouldn't allow himself to fully participate in the event. A double-blind test is designed to objectify the process to ensure validity. We are actually doing the opposite. We want to get *past* objectivity to ensure validity. It demands that you participate fully.

The people he "tested" it on had just been introduced to this new idea, and were easily distracted from their nascent coherence. Many of us are tempted to "test" our coherence prematurely, and abandon it before it is ready for primetime.

For instance, if you are teaching little Susie how to kick a soccer ball, you won't get far by "proving" that she is incapable of doing it right. There are a thousand ways to fail, and she doesn't need to experience them all. Susie will learn much faster if you patiently guide her. To succeed, you must be fully engaged…in the moment. If she tries to kick the ball "like last time," she won't be here with *this ball*, this time.

There are also a thousand ways to do this exercise wrong, and most of them have to do with how you objectify what you are doing. But, since that is what it is designed to correct, persistence in the exercise will overcome that eventually.

Ready to give it a whirl?

A single event can awaken within us a stranger totally unknown to us. To live is to be slowly born.

Antoine de Saint-Exupéry

Chapter 16
Instant Meditation

We meditate to find, to recover, to come back to something of ourselves we once dimly and unknowingly had and have lost without knowing what it was or where or when we lost it.

Lawrence LeShan

I discovered the pointing-finger technique for heightening coherence in my martial arts. It improved my speed, power, presence, reaction time, and balance. That was quite a lot already. But all that directed me to more universal applications. We'll be getting to those in the remainder of this book.

Since a firm foundation in coherence is essential for all that follows, I ask that you actually *do* the following exercises, not just read about them.

There are ways to do this by yourself, but it's better with a partner that understands what you are trying to accomplish. Skip the know-it-all jerk who just wants to show you how dumb you are for even trying something this crazy. You want someone with a modicum of curiosity. Otherwise, practice it yourself and then test it on unsuspecting random individuals.

Exercise: Pointing for Coherence

Do the following in super slow motion. That will give you an opportunity to tune into the subtleties of the process. Nothing will

101

be learned by using abrupt movements at the start. When you can successfully and confidently apply it slowly, then gradually increase the speed.

Part One

1. Have your partner stand in a relaxed posture. She extends her hand as if to shake hands. Grab her wrist and slowly push her arm toward the center of her body. Ask her to resist with her muscles. Gradually increase the pressure until the arm goes back. Ask her to note her level of effort. (Note: This establishes your baseline of muscular resistance. You want a fairly weak muscular connection, one that collapses without too much effort. If this one is too strong, have her hold her arm parallel with the chest about six inches away.)

2. Ask her to assume the same starting position, but this time to point and reach toward your chest as though she were going to touch it. "Reaching" implies extending with intention, like pointing to a pastry in a bakery to say, "I want that one." You are not just pushing your hand out. There is an intention.

3. Back to the starting position. Grab her wrist and ask her to repeat the action in Step 2 above, but this time you gradually increase the force on her arm. She reaches even more as you increase the pressure. Ask her to notice the significant increase in her ability to hold her position.

4. Try this several times. Notice that her effective power increased dramatically when pointing and reaching with intention. There was also a powerful attraction to the earth that far exceeded her normal sense of "balance." In t'ai chi ch'uan terms, pointing and reaching with focused attention has made her internal energy, her qi (pronounced chee), more coherent. Her body-mind displayed qualities unavailable in its more non-coherent state.

The earth-connection is called *rooting*. Her coherence allowed her to enhance her resonance with the larger energy field of the earth and thus create a greater attraction.

Practice many times. This is a new skill. It requires a conscious decision again and again to overcome established patterns.

Part Two

Once you get the feeling of enhanced coherence and begin to trust the power that comes with it, try this:

1.   Have her point to establish her coherence. Push on her wrist to confirm it for both of you.
2.   Now ask her to "think about her finger." Test this. Notice that "thinking about" her finger has made her weaker. Someone let the air out of the tire. Why? Her coherence (Wholeness) is disrupted. To think about her finger, she had to separate out from it and render her body into a mind-object.
3.   Ask her to re-establish coherence by *feeling* her finger (as opposed to thinking about it) as she points and reaches. It may help for her to wiggle it to get her attention there again.
4.   Try it a few times to overcome the natural skepticism that comes from encountering something new and strange.

I have shared this with thousands of people and when they see the implications...well, minds are blown. It's a little like finding out that painting you got for $50 at the garage sale is not just a really good Picasso copy. It's still the same canvas, but you regard it with different eyes now.

When coherent, consciousness pervades the body. In a non-coherent state, there is a tendency to think of the body as something separate, an object to be used, endured, or even punished. Some religions consider the body evil, and regard mutilation, flagellation, and asceticism as swell ideas.

Non-coherence is the source of many mental and physical problems. In my practice I have seen that many of them disappear unaddressed, simply by heightening coherence. The body-mind likes Wholeness and works to bring itself into a more optimal state. When exposed to Wholeness, old patterns can be shed if they seem deleterious.

Pointing is like using a key to start a car. Imagine you've never heard of an automobile before and someone shows you this structure of metal, glass, plastic, and rubber sitting there, and then says that this small, flat piece of metal (a key) will make magical things happen. "What sort of magic?" you ask. "This piece of metal will make it go faster than the wind, heat up or cool off the space inside, and play music, among other things." "Sounds crazy to me," you say, "Let's see it."

Turning the key in the ignition brings this ton of resting metal into a heightened state of coherence. The computer comes on and now the car can do all sorts of amazing things. We haven't added new hardware to make this happen. It comes from accessing a higher order of coherence. And that requires energy and information.

Energetic Coherence

Arthur C. Clarke's famous "Laws of Prediction" guide us in our explorations:

1. When a distinguished but elderly scientist states that something is possible, he is almost certainly right. When he states that something is impossible, he is very probably wrong.
2. The only way of discovering the limits of the possible is to venture a little way past them into the impossible.
3. Any sufficiently advanced technology is indistinguishable from magic.

Thinking about coherence as a scientist might, we consider it as the relative order within any system.

Coherence is not just a physical phenomenon; energy can also be coherent. *Energetic coherence* is the degree that waves align in frequency, amplitude, direction, and phase. Instead of crashing together and neutralizing their effect, the coherent waves amplify each other. The classic example is the laser, which is coherent light. In its coherent state, light is capable of much more than the dispersed photons of an ordinary incandescent bulb—delicate surgeries, for example.

Similarly, when the bioenergy of your body-mind (qi, ch'i, prana, elan vital) is brought into Wholeness by your consciousness…well, cool things happen. This is what makes Chinese internal martial arts work, as well as acupuncture and other forms of energy medicine, and some types of yoga. Energy and information are organized in ways that enable us to perform strange and seemingly miraculous feats.

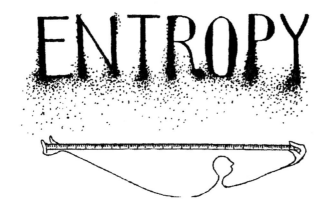

Entropy—the amount of randomness and disorder in a system—is inversely proportional to coherence. When there is a lot of disorder, energy is expended inefficiently. That means that energy loss in any system will be less if it is optimally organized. Your body seems to age slower if it is more coherent.

Entropy is like leaks in a rowboat. Instead of skimming lightly on the water, there is now a lot of water in the boat. You are pulling the weight of the water now too. It takes more energy to move. And when you have a leaky boat, fixing the problem becomes your top priority. Patch the holes and Wholeness is restored.

Wholeness gives you the peace of mind to consider other possibilities. It opens you to your creative nature. It provides the foundation for body-mind-spirit integration. Too much non-coherence and all you can think about is your leaky boat.

Instant Meditation

It's hard to imagine Wholeness when deep in the It-trance. Your mind churns constantly trying to solve the riddle of non-coherence. And that feeds back on itself and generates more non-coherence. You have trouble clearing your mind to sleep well at night.

Regular practice of meditation can certainly help. There is ample documentation for that. Slowing the "monkey mind" allows us to see that there are alternatives to the churning and grasping of a divided intellect.

The biggest barrier to meditation is that we lose heart before the good stuff kicks in. And having failed a few times to get there, we are less inclined to sit uncomfortably without something to amuse and distract. Only the most robust (or desperate) among us are willing to log the hours. The following practice helps to cut through all that and get us to "the good part."

Instant Meditation: Sitting

How about we start with you sitting in a comfy chair. Turn the TV off. Phone on mute. Soft music if it's not too distracting. How's that? Now take a couple of slow, deep breaths just to remember that breathing is a really swell idea and that you should continue to do it. For many reasons.

The key to this technique is to actually feel your index fingers when you point and reach with them. Feel them from "inside" your body. Wiggle them, and notice that the ones you move feel different from the ones you don't move. You are not just thinking about them.

Imagine you are reaching for a light switch. That's the amount of muscular tension you want. Not too tense, but enough to remind you that those fingers are part of you and will do things if you ask them nicely.

Notice the sensations in your hand after a few seconds. You might feel vibrations or heat in your hands, and then in other parts of your body as you connect up. It's faint, but you can learn to detect it. Feel what is happening, but don't get caught up in the story. Notice it then move on to the next moment.

Now extend your awareness to your mind. Notice your thoughts have calmed down. The normal chatter of your everyday thinking mind recedes as it is replaced by the events of the moment. Now.

"Your mind will seek to configure a story"

Your mind will seek to configure a story about them and take you back onto more familiar ground. Don't resist this. Just notice it, relax your fingers, and then point again. Feel your fingers. Anew.

It only takes a second to clear your thoughts. You are not your thoughts. When a thought dissolves into the Mystery from whence it came, you are still here to witness as the next one arises. The It-trance is suspended for the moment.

Repeat. For a few moments. Or minutes. Or as long as you like. It gets easier. It's also cumulative, added to your account at the First Natural Bank of Consciousness. At first, the space between thoughts may only be a tiny crack, but with practice it gets bigger. And bigger.

Once you get the hang of it, you can try it anywhere, any time. It's easy. It costs nothing. You usually take your fingers with you wherever you go. It can take as little as two seconds to get some coherence going.

Shoot for a hundred times a day. It just takes a few seconds to make the shift. It calms your nervous system and focuses your mind. As I mentioned, the effect is cumulative. If you do it a hundred times a day for a week you will likely experience a significant, persistent improvement in body-mind-spirit integration.

Cool stuff happens.

Space Between Thoughts

In the gap between thoughts, non-conceptual wisdom shines continuously.

Milarepa

When you are highly coherent, it becomes easier to tap into an ocean of non-conceptual awareness. It is without shape or form. No thought, feeling, or perception. No-thing. Emptiness. Our thoughts are waves that appear and disappear on its surface. Through a practice like meditation, we begin to notice the difference between differentiated and undifferentiated mind-states.

Our thoughts may appear to come in a continuous stream, one after another, but that is not really accurate. Each thought that comes to mind has a beginning, a middle, and an end. It arises in the nervous system, gets the attention of the conscious mind, and then goes away. And before and after each thought there is a space…a *no-thought*. If you are already entranced by the next thought that appears, you may not notice this space. But it was there, however briefly.

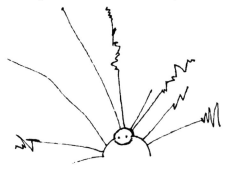

"Space between thoughts"

This *space between thoughts* is the same space we encountered in the abstraction cycle discussed in Chapter Ten. It is that moment of awareness in any event *before we begin the process of abstraction…* even before we consider there is an object to conceptualize. It is a moment of objectless awareness, a moment before we begin constructing a narrative about the event.

The It-mind does not usually consider that moment of non-thinking valuable. It prefers instantaneous inference about what is going on. Quick thinking is a highly regarded skill in a world exploding in information, and most of our education is geared to developing cognitive ability.

We can have both. We need both.

Meditation is anything that helps us differentiate thought/no thought by training our attention. With practice, we awaken from the It-trance, ready to participate fully in our lives.

Meditation is the dissolution of thoughts in Eternal awareness or Pure consciousness without objectification, knowing without thinking, merging finitude in infinity.

Voltaire

Chapter 17
What's in It for Me?

When you change the way you look at things, the things you are looking at change.

Max Planck

Let's pause a moment and consider the practical benefits of enhancing energetic coherence. Some of them have been mentioned, but that information could easily be overlooked or forgotten.

Here are some questions that arise:

Q. My life is really busy right now. I understand that accessing heightened coherence takes but a second or two and the effects can be really powerful, but I still don't see where it fits in my life. Can you give me some concrete examples?

A. Most of us won't take deliberate steps to change our way of doing things unless there's a really good reason. Even something as small as pointing a finger may seem too much of a bother if we don't expect a substantial payday.

So what can we actually expect from a regular practice of improving coherence?

Let's start with health and longevity. If there is a reasonable expectation that you will be healthier and live longer, is that motivation?

Ervin Laszlo wrote, "Living organisms are complex systems in a state far from thermodynamic equilibrium. They need to meet stringent conditions for maintaining themselves in their physically improbable and inherently unstable condition."

When those stringent conditions are met and things are working smoothly, we are coherent. We humans are uniquely challenged in that we create most of our own coherence and non-coherence...ourselves... by the narratives we construct.

Coherent systems don't wear out as fast as non-coherent ones. Entropy can be considered as energy loss or the tendency for complex systems to break down. A car badly in need of a tune up and oil change is non-coherent. It wastes gas, wears out prematurely, and is a lousy ride. Bad diet, poor sleeping habits, and tense muscles all create non-coherence in the body-mind. So does worry or anger.

One main reason why t'ai chi (taijiquan) has the reputation of enhancing health and longevity is that, when done properly, it enhances coherence. Symphony conductors also seem to live long, active lives. Again, I believe that coherence is a big part of that. When coherent, your body-mind works better...at least in the long run.

You can get some outstanding performance by just pushing yourself to the limit, but that's a bad long-term strategy. If it generates entropy, your body-mind will wear out faster. Getting more coherent in your body-mind and also with your environment enables peak performance and also reduces stress on the system.

Q. Is the ideal to be coherent all the time?

A. No. To be clear, you are coherent just by being alive. Coherence is a quality of all living creatures. Life organizes inert matter into systems that function as entities and can reproduce. We are actually talking here about increasing the level of coherence, short term and long term, to improve all aspects of your life.

You familiarize yourself with enhanced coherence through practice over time. It's an acquired taste and not how we are used to existing. Some people think they function better in a state of near-hysteria. And they may... short term. But constant stress and hyper-vigilance will lead to many of the physical, emotional, and mental problems that beset our culture.

The ideal is to gradually raise the baseline of coherence so that we can effectively deal with the challenges of life with effortless competence. From this higher baseline, it becomes easier to move to "superhuman" levels for short periods.

Q. Is there a time when we want to be more *non*-coherent?

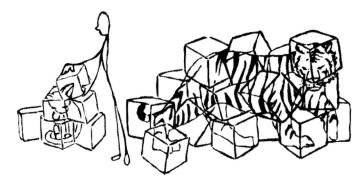

A. Absolutely. Coherence is an attribute of Wholeness. We are better able to DO from that state. But life is not just about the doing. We humans also like to think about stuff, and that means breaking things down into pieces and putting them back together in creative ways.

One has to be *non-coherent* to some degree to learn or create anything new. You must break the proverbial eggs to make an omelet. Each transformation includes a stage of chaos, where things are seemingly unpredictable. That chaos is the birthplace of new structures.

Knowing how to easily return to coherence allows us to confidently go even deeper into that creative chaos.

Q. Should I just walk around with my fingers pointed all the time?

A. That's not going to work, and besides, it would look pretty dumb. Coherence is not restored merely by the position of the index finger. *It is activated by bringing consciousness to the process.* You have to reach with the finger, feel the sensations that arise, and KNOW that you are doing it. If you point your finger and forget that you are doing so, the body-mind-spirit integration evaporates.

It also disappears if you think *about* your finger. That puts you back in the It-mind. The alternative that we cultivate through this process is the non-objective awareness discussed earlier. At first, that state is hard to discern, but with practice it becomes as familiar as your own skin. And, like your skin, you don't notice it until you notice it.

Q. So when is the best time to practice?

A. Any time and any place. I recommend that you do it a hundred times a day. Get used to finding coherence in non-stressful situations so that the confidence is there when you need it to handle the big challenges.

As mentioned in Chapter Sixteen, pointing is like the key that starts your car. You put the key in the ignition with the intention to activate a higher level of functioning. The car's computer starts, the engine fires up, the lights come on, the radio plays—none of that is happening until you activate it by turning the key.

Q. I'm anxious much of the time. I can't stop this barrage of negative thoughts. Can coherence help me calm down?

A. It does for many. Fear does not happen in a highly coherent state. Your mind clears almost immediately, so there is nothing left to fear.

Anxiety is fear of an imagined future. The stuff you are anxious about does not exist, and may never come to pass. Anxiety becomes a non-specific fear of everything. In extreme cases, your thoughts can freeze you into terrified inaction.

We all have the ability to imagine a lot of terrible things that could happen. One of the characteristics that have allowed humans to survive as a species is the ability to anticipate

"Pointing is the key that starts your car"

danger. However, the responses that alerted our predecessors to the dangers of wild animals and attacking warriors don't serve us as well when dealing with scowling bosses and impatient teenagers.

Fear is highly non-coherent. It disrupts Wholeness. Non-coherence alerts the nervous system that something is wrong. We want to feel whole and so look for the source of the disruption everywhere, but all we find are ghosts. This creates more non-coherence, more disruption, more ghosts.

We solve this by increasing coherence. Coherence calms the nervous system. Our worries start to dissolve immediately. If the It-mind tries to revive them, we point again and clear the mind, find the space between thoughts. Each time we do it, it becomes easier to do. Anxiety disappears. If it returns, you repeat the process.

Q. I guess that is true for negative self-criticism too.

A. Yes, coherence helps us control any form of unwanted negative thinking. Obsessive self-criticism has its root in the objectification of self. To denigrate our own self we must first imagine it as a separate object with objectionable attributes.

This is a good clue that you are deep in the It-trance. It might be time to take a break and get highly coherent for a while. Coherence creates some room to breathe. In later chapters we will discuss how to easily shift into a relational mode of being. That offers a desirable alternative to beating yourself up.

Q. You gave a recipe for *Instant Meditation,* and it is effective. What happens when I practice that for a longer period of time?

A. Instant Meditation gets us over the initial hurdle of clearing the mind. The next challenge is acclimating to the space between thoughts. If you are deep in the It-trance, a clear, calm mind may be unrecognizable at first. We can get quite addicted to our little dramas, and quickly fill the void when threatened with peace.

Persistence is rewarded, however. You can practice Instant Meditation anytime you have two or three seconds to calm your mind. Even better when you do it for five or fifteen minutes...or longer. The effects are cumulative.

Q. When I practice Instant Meditation, my mind does clear. But then the thoughts and the worries return. Is there a way to produce a more stable state?

A. Thoughts will return. Expect that. It's something we humans like to do.

Now you get to choose which thoughts you want to entertain.

You want to be able to think rationally whenever you choose, to access the operating system that is appropriate for the moment, and to shift quickly and smoothly between them.

That is much harder when you are deep in the It-trance.

The It-trance runs on automatic for most of us, so finding the off-switch is essential. Until you learn to control your attention, it is all too easy to succumb to the sub-conscious programs that dominate most behavior. The non-objective state becomes more stable once you learn to like it more than the drama-filled reactivity of the It-trance.

Q. I already practice a meditation. Will it conflict with this one?

A. I can't think of any form of meditation that would not be enhanced by heightened coherence. It brings you into a state of Wholeness and allows you to do whatever you are doing with the fullness of your being.

With practice, your body-mind becomes a fertile ground for peace and serenity. You bring more of your attention into the present moment easily and often. It is only in the Present that we truly Live.

I cannot be awake for nothing looks to me as it did before,
Or else I am awake for the first time, and all before has been a
mean sleep.

Walt Whitman

Chapter 18
Presence

Throughout my whole life, during every minute of it, the world has been gradually lighting up and blazing before my eyes until it has come to surround me, entirely lit up from within.

Pierre Teilhard de Chardin

It all begins with Presence.

Before we can engage life fully, before we can meet another with our whole being, an important choice must be made. It is the decision to Be...to personally assume a position in space and time. It is the most courageous decision we can make, for no choices are our own until we do.

It means to take responsibility for the moment you are actually in, and not act from your ideas about some other time, past or future. It is not enough to be here in body only, with attention elsewhere. Nor is it enough to just be present as "observer" or "witness," detached from self and other.

We encounter with our whole being.

Presence embraces What-is, and What-is also includes the being that is me. I can only participate to the degree that I am willing to Be.

"Take responsibility for the moment you are actually in"

We may take existence for granted, but true Presence is actually pretty rare. Most of our attention ordinarily focuses on making sense of what we think is happening,

115

has happened, and might happen. Presence arises when we bring attention to What-is without explanation.

Paradoxically, all our efforts to understand what's going on now take us out of Now, if even for a moment. We can't think about some thing or some one unless we first step back for a moment and objectify it. It must be abstracted, flattened out, and rendered into symbols that can be identified, organized, counted, and compared. Of course, this is that most indispensable of human qualities: our ability to tell a story. We don't survive very long (or very happily) if we are unable to string our random perceptions into a meaningful narrative.

It is only by embracing our dual nature that we know wisdom, satisfaction, and love in the lived life.

There is an inside and an outside to everything, including our "self." Alan Watts wrote,

> *Really, the fundamental, ultimate mystery—the only thing you need to know to understand the deepest metaphysical secrets—is this: that for every outside there is an inside and for every inside there is an outside, and although they are different, they go together.*

The outside of the self is how it appears…my experience of "me." My ego. The inside of the self has no objective aspects, no qualities, no story.

Presence includes both inner and outer aspects. We must know who and what we are in order to play any sort of game, even the game of living as a two-legger on a blue-green planet.

The ego is like our marker in a game of *Monopoly.* It tells us where we are in the game. Yet our most cherished moments are those seen from the inside, when our attention shifts primarily to the *play* of the game itself, not how it appears. It is then that our story disappears for the moment and there is only Now.

Until we consciously embrace the moment we are in, we are but two-dimensional characters in a narrative of our own fabrication. Unless we play those roles as free beings, conscious of our choice, they have no actuality. It is the difference between riding a bike and watching an edited video of yourself riding.

Our ability to participate in all that life has to offer is directly proportional to our willingness to (in the famous rallying cry of Ram Dass) *"Be Here Now."*

It is a decision we make again and again. Do I play or do I watch? Do I just go through the motions or do I engage life as if it matters? As if *I* matter? Like a shy teenager at a dance, I can cocoon myself in my narrative until the music is over and I didn't once get out on the floor. Or I can steel my courage and seize the moment.

Carpe occasionem!

Controlling Attention

The conventional (I-It) use of the word "presence" is, "the state or fact of existing or occurring in a place or thing." This is a simple way to state that some object is in the proximity of the observer. That object can be another human or even yourself. It speaks of our *experience* of the thing being spoken *about:* its qualities and appearance. It locates one object by comparing it to another.

When a schoolteacher calls roll to ask the implied question, "Are you present?" it is essentially to determine if the student brought a body to class that day. The student's *attention* is optional.

But true Presence requires that we freely bring our attention into Now. This is something that does not register with the I-It OS, because "attention" and "Now" are not objects. However, the It-mind can see their effects, just as it can tell an airplane has passed by noting the jet contrail. The It-mind will happily follow the vapor trails left by events gone by or speculate on the imagined events of an undetermined future until we actually make the choice to embrace What-is.

Presence asks, "How much am I willing to be in *this* place at *this* time doing what I'm doing? How much awareness do I bring to this moment?"

"Nursing remembered or imagined wounds"

The ability to control attention is crucial. For someone floundering in a mental maelstrom of negativity, this may seem an impossible task. Thoughts seem to arise of their own accord. If you are deep in the It-trance, thoughts can have as much actuality as a punch in the nose. You can still be nursing remembered or imagined wounds decades later.

To truly know that *you are not your thoughts* is to free yourself from their thrall. That requires knowing the space between thoughts.

At first, controlling attention may be as difficult as catching a trout with salad tongs. Your mind seems to have a mind of its own. But you can start by setting the conditions to succeed.

A recovering alcoholic knows that his proximity to liquor leads inevitably to consumption, so he is resolute about avoiding situations where he will be tempted. He puts space between himself and his demons. I may be too torpid on a hot summer day to conceive of practicing my martial arts, but if I can coax myself to do "just a couple minutes" I often will keep on going. The distance between zero and one is greater than between one and a hundred. Just getting on my feet creates the conditions that make a workout possible.

One important condition we can learn to control is our own energetic coherence. Instant Meditation is a quick, dependable way to bring yourself into the present moment by heightening body-mind coherence. If you didn't get a chance to do the exercise thoroughly, take some time now to check it out. It is something that should be done quite often (I recommend a hundred times a day) to get the feeling. Unless you participate in Instant Meditation, it is just another abstraction and not the useful tool for establishing Presence that it can be.

Each time you heighten your coherence it becomes easier to maintain. Eventually, higher levels of coherence become your preferred states.

Many of us give up on meditation too soon because we are unable to quiet our minds long enough to feel any progress. We may try to "not think," and that only makes matters worse since now we are "thinking about not thinking."

Mental noise is a by-product of a non-coherent state. The nervous system recognizes that something is out of synch and tenaciously tries to solve this riddle. It rummages through our ongoing narrative to explain the discomfort of non-coherence.

It bears repeating that the actual solution lies in heightening body-mind coherence. When we do that, we actually re-integrate body, mind, and spirit. We shift from objectification of ourselves (where we have created psychic distance from our own selves) to a state of unity where such objectification dissolves.

In terms of our present discussion, it could be said that by pointing and feeling the index finger, we are shifting from an *experience* (I-It) of the body-mind to *relating* to the body-mind (I-You) as a partner. Relating bridges the gap created by "experiencing" the body as something separate: "too fat, too thin, too tired, too old, etc." A kind of alchemy occurs when relating, and what was experienced as separateness re-integrates and returns to Wholeness.

It may seem weird to think about relating to the body as a partner, particularly if you consider it as a biomechanical device that is the source of so much consternation and disappointment. Coherence dissolves that arbitrary separation and heals the source of so many physical and mental woes.

Instant Meditation is an effective tool, and I recommend doing it before beginning any task (including the exercises in this book.) There is no substitute for actually doing it...often and well. It establishes a foundation of Wholeness for engaging the world.

In the next chapter, we take Presence one step further by examining ways to locate a self lost in the confusing turbulence of the It-trance.

Contemplation amidst activity is a thousand million times superior to contemplation in stillness.

Hakuin, Zen master (1685-1768)

Chapter 19

Locating Yourself

The present moment is a powerful goddess.

Goethe

Presence is attention in the Now and Here. How much do I wish to participate in this moment?

If our thoughts take us elsewhere, how present can we be?

If I am preparing for karaoke or to toast the bride and groom, and all I can think of is times I failed or embarrassed myself, am I really here doing what I'm doing? If I continue to argue in my mind long after a conversation is over, where am I exactly?

For many of us, our thoughts are sometimes runaway trains—we can only watch them and try not to be crushed. Other times they slowly erode our peace

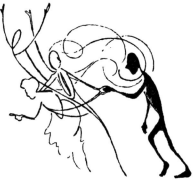

"If our thoughts take us elsewhere, how present can we be?"

of mind by keeping us in a slow boil of regret, dissatisfaction, or resentment.

It is easy to get caught in a loop: about how life fails to meet our expectations, how we've been injured by the actions or inactions of others, or by things we did or said that continue to haunt us. We hope to find the answer to our unease in the past or future, and the old tapes play over and over.

In actuality, it is only by understanding and embracing our current condition (whatever it may be) that we can make true and effective changes for the better. Most of us have some mental noise pulling our attention in different directions, and it is all too easy to let it take over and sabotage our best efforts. Learning to control attention means somehow filtering out unnecessary thinking in order to bring more awareness to the task at hand.

In the movie *For the Love of the Game,* Kevin Costner plays an aging baseball pitcher trying to keep his career going a little longer. He goes to the mound and is aware of crowd noise and the many distractions that could throw off his game.

When he's ready to throw, however, he shifts his awareness and "engages the mechanism." That is his name for a mental process that filters out everything but the job he's there to do. The camera gives us a first-person perspective of his change in perception. The crowd noise fades to a whisper and his entire focus goes to the ball, batter, catcher, and umpire. Nothing else matters during that time.

How exactly does he "engage the mechanism?" We never learn that from the movie. Maybe the pitcher himself can't explain it. But all great athletes have some process they use to help them be more present at crucial times. Those who can't control their attention may get a reputation for choking under pressure.

Since we were children we have been coaxed, bullied, extolled, instructed, and reminded to "pay attention." To be Present, we must be able to control our minds.

Wild animals that are not aware of their circumstances tend to be someone's supper. Human groups protect their inattentive members… up to a point. Adults who have no control of their attention have difficulty functioning. Some are dangerous. For a sentry in a war zone or a surgeon making a delicate cut, attention is crucial.

If Joe is texting on his iPhone while driving a busy street, he may not notice the pedestrian stepping in front of his car. Joe may be present with his smartphone, but not so much with the driving part of the program.

We cut children some slack, hoping they'll develop the ability to keep their minds on the task at hand. Part of the maturation process is to learn to attend to your responsibilities, thus repaying your tribe for its indulgence. This means actually showing up for whatever it is you are doing.

In my work as a Polarity therapist I don't have the luxury of inattention. The work requires that one be centered and focused from the start of a session and be able to maintain that for hours. I work with my clients' energy fields and must be aware of subtle fluctuations in something many people have no awareness of. There is no time in the session to go wandering in the labyrinth of idle thoughts. My effectiveness depends on the ability to Be. Here. Now.

Presence takes practice. We all stumble in and out of it, but to be able to sustain it or access it while under pressure is a special skill. Decades of practice have given me some insight into how to direct and sustain attention. It's actually quite simple.

But simple doesn't mean it's easy.

Mindfulness

The most precious gift we can offer others is our presence. When mindfulness embraces those we love, they will bloom like flowers.

Thich Nhat Hanh

Mindfulness is the practice of moment-by-moment awareness of thoughts, feelings, bodily sensations, and surroundings. We pull our attention from the bouillabaisse of past and future and bring the mind to Now. There is no time to think about what is happening because the next moment is here and it needs our full awareness.

Meditation is the traditional tool for developing this ability. We quiet the muddy mental waters and allow the silt to settle. There are many types of meditation, but most follow that formula: quiet the mind and let the noise evaporate.

This is a basic method for learning to control thoughts. By placing a priority on counting breaths, for instance, other thoughts are weeded out. When the interlopers crash the party, one simply returns to counting breaths. Those mental gatecrashers will just have to wait.

Or, one can control attention by witnessing thoughts as they arise without attaching importance to them. Too many are labeled, "Urgent! SOS! Handle immediately!" and are backed by physiological cattle prods designed to command our attention. They trigger an artificial state of emergency that uses fear to push to the head of the line.

This hypervigilence is a vestige from our remote past that aided survival when threats required immediate physical solutions. Life in the twenty-first century calls for more nuanced responses than "fight, flight, or freeze"—yet the old system still colors our lives. It continues to do so until we take it off automatic.

Notice the thoughts without getting caught up in their drama. Then notice the space between the thoughts. Thoughts arise, and then go away. Like a parent patiently waiting for a child's tantrum to subside, we can calm this flow simply by refusing to take the bait.

"Thoughts arise and then go away"

The mental noise clears and we become aware that there is an interval between our thoughts. In that space the mind becomes clear and calm, at first for moments, and then for longer periods. Regular practice allows us to become familiar with this clear mind state and we gradually come to expect it.

When your thoughts no longer control you, you can learn to control them.

Finding Yourself

After these things, God tested Avraham. He said to him, "Avraham!" And he answered, "Here I am."

Genesis 22-1, Complete Jewish Bible

If presence is indeed tied to attention, then it's a good idea to reclaim as much attention as we can.

Many of us have great bunches of mind-stuff stuck in past traumas and losses that suck us in like black holes, so meandering about in our memories will take us even farther from now. One thought leads to another and soon we are arguing with dad about denting the car when we were sixteen or crying about a beloved pet that died twenty years ago.

Or we imagine all sorts of dreadful possible futures that trigger the same fears that actual events do. When we follow a thought down the rabbit hole, we don't know where it will lead. It can be a source of creative inspiration when channeled correctly. When we have no control over our thoughts for an extended period we lose ourselves in our thoughts.

When lost, it is usually a good idea to find your bearings. Ordinarily, we locate ourselves by noticing objects and orienting to them. "I'm in the backyard in the hammock," for example, or "I'm at the office thinking about the project due tomorrow." We derive the location of the "me-object" by comparing it to other objects. This is something we are doing more or less constantly as we update the story we tell ourselves.

While this helps us get our story straight, we need a different tool—one that brings us into the present moment with greater clarity. Instead of deriving our location by the objects in our surroundings, we locate ourselves by the true north of NOW and HERE. We intentionally shift from the I-It OS by locating ourselves non-objectively.

Instant Presence

A fast, easy way to stop chasing random thoughts is to simply locate yourself non-objectively by asking:
"Where am I now?" (You don't need to say this aloud.)
There is only one answer: "Here I am."
As in:
Where am I now?
Here I am.
No objects. No story. Just a simple statement of *non-objective* time/space location.
Who is here?
I am.
Where am I?
Here.
When am I?
Now.

You are not seeking information. You are not telling yourself a story about what is happening and where.

Instead, it is a statement of your *decision* to occupy this space at this moment. You take control of attention and bring it to Now. You put aside for the moment all those thoughts and memories *about* things and decide to just BE.

It is like refreshing a computer display. You are saying, "Regardless of how I got to this place, here is where I am." Reset!

(There is time later to review what happened and note the lessons learned, but you must be able to *not* do that as well—and simply act effectively from a state of Wholeness in the present moment.)

Do it with the same sense of playful discovery as in a game of peekaboo with a toddler. What are we saying to the child when we play that game? "I don't see you. Where did you go? You are not present. Oh, Now I see you! Here you are! I am so happy!"

Please note that the answer to the question, "Where am I?" is, "Here I Am." It is not, "I'm here" or "Here." Those answers are I-It responses and don't do exactly what we want.

"Here. I. Am." It is decisive. There is definiteness about this response that says "I am present and available for whatever life has to offer."

When we do it, we reconnect with the flow of the universe in that moment, and in some small way reaffirm our connection to Spirit. We resonate with What-is, and in doing so we draw upon power much greater than our own.

Presence in Action

Cindy is a dog trainer in California. To bring some order into her class of canines and their humans, she asked her *Homo sapiens* students to respond to roll call by emphatically answering, "Here I am!" The results were amazing. Both dogs and humans responded eagerly to increased Presence in the room. The one time she forgot to do it, she said the class was chaotic and frustrating.

I enjoy golf, although I rarely play more than a couple times a year. I'm a double-bogey player (averaging two over par per hole) on a good day. A duffer. Golf demands a samurai-like focus on each shot to be effective, and sternly punishes inattention. If I am still celebrating a great putt on the last hole or frustrated by several bad tee shots, then I'm not really present with the shot I need to make now.

So when I played recently, I tried to firmly establish my presence for each shot. I would take a deep breath, relax, and then point and reach my index fingers. Then I'd clear my mind of all other considerations by locating myself in the moment by asking, "Where am I now?" and answering, "Here I am!"

My strokes became relaxed and easy, yet powerful and accurate. It was the best round I had played in twenty years. In the past, I would have moments of clarity, but this was the first time I consciously established presence as my first order of business for each new shot.

I find the best strategy for most activities is to establish a baseline of presence by performing these two actions as often as I think of them. I point my index fingers to enhance Wholeness and ask "Where am I now?" to affirm Presence.

You want to be so familiar with the state that you notice when you get caught up in mental turbulence. So maybe you do it once a minute for a while.

When playing tennis, I try to clear the buffer after each point until I'm well established in a calm, energized state. So even when I lose it, I know it's not far away.

On a long car ride, I'll pull myself back from a mental excursion by asking the magic question. Nervous about a presentation you have to give? Be the most present one in the room and see how that goes.

These are two rugged, predictable, versatile tools for establishing and enhancing presence in virtually any situation. Point and reach first to establish optimal conditions for success. Then locate yourself in this place and this time.

Like anything new, this ability to reset our awareness needs to be learned diligently over time. While powerful, it is also subtle. In music it is as important to hear the spaces between notes as the notes themselves. We are attuning ourselves to the spaces between thoughts, thereby transforming how we think and act. With practice it can be performed by our higher mind faster than we can even notice.

When you are present, you can allow the mind to be as it is without getting entangled in it. The mind in itself is a wonderful tool. Dysfunction sets in when you seek your self in it and mistake it for who you are.

Eckhart Tolle

Chapter 20

Where Are You Now?

Love gives naught but itself and takes naught but from itself.
Love possesses not nor would it be possessed;
For love is sufficient unto love.

Kahlil Gibran, poet

The two pre-conditions to Finding You in a World of It are Wholeness and Presence. A system functions better in a state of Wholeness. Presence resets our minds from a whirlwind of random thoughts to focus on this place and this time.

For many, it is enough to be whole, present, and mindful—and some may consider it to be the pinnacle of human achievement. Some spiritual practices exalt the image of a blissed-out yogi, smiling beatifically in an unending *satori* of pure unattached, uninvolved awareness.

If that is your cup of tea, go for it. Shave your head and retreat to a nice ashram somewhere where this crazy world of ours doesn't intrude into your *unio mystica*.

For the rest of us who actually prefer the lived life—participatory consciousness—Wholeness and presence are not the end goal; they are the beginning.

That is where the fun begins. We can play.

The game doesn't start until you show up ready to play. Just being and witnessing are not enough. The depth, fullness, richness, and authenticity we find in living come from engaging the world and its inhabitants.

129

There is an ongoing dance of relation and experience in all parts of our lives, requiring that we be both present with our dance partner(s) and cognizant of the dance being performed. I relate to You, and then step back to sort out what just happened. Some small part of the event may be remembered as experience. Repeat as desired.

Buber says it best:

> *When I confront a human being as my You and speak the basic word I-You to him, then he is no thing among things nor does he consist of things. He is no longer He or She, limited by other Hes and Shes, a dot in the world grid of space and time, nor a condition that can be experienced and described, a loose bundle of named qualities. Neighborless and seamless, he is You and fills the firmament. Not as if there were nothing but he; but everything else lives in his light.*

To play the game, to dance the dance, to know what it means to be really alive…you need partners. I must find You. The form that You takes doesn't matter: human, animal, plant, mineral, ghost, sonnet, energy, or god. It only matters that I meet You with my whole being, not as if there were nothing but You, but everything lives in Your light. We operate, we play, from Wholeness and Presence.

How do we shift from the you of "that loose bundle of named qualities" to the one You that "fills the firmament?" How do we tap into that divine electricity that surges between I and You?

The answer is surprisingly simple. But to get beyond the walls that separate us from each other, we need to know a few things about boundaries.

Making and Unmaking Boundaries

Boundaries are established by thoughts. Maps need them to say, "this is not that."

We need partners. I must find You.

The It-mind sets boundaries and adds to existing ones. Relation transcends or dissolves them.

To experience something, we separate it out from other things, if only by identifying it. Boundaries separate things and also connect them in the way we think about them. Life pulses between separation and connection. The one that is real for us in the moment is the one we focus on.

For example, when I smell a rose I am reminded that the rose and I are separate. I am here and it is there. There is a barrier of space between us, but that begins to change when I become conscious of our separateness. The rose has reached out with some of its molecules to caress my olfactories. I perceive those molecules as a delightful aroma.

Rose particles have already mingled with my body, and that blurs the boundary between us. Paradoxically, the very thing that alerts me to this external object as something other than me is also the thing that connects us.

When I think about the rose, I am separate from it. When I engage the rose as a partner in an intoxicating love-fest, there is no separation.

It is in bridging the apparent gap between us that pleasure is taken. The enjoyment diminishes if I am overexposed to that scent—or any other—because there is no separation to overcome.

There is no one perfect state or condition that we can grasp and hold. We derive pleasure by reuniting after separation, not by continued immersion in even the most blissful of circumstances.

Relating dissolves boundaries…temporarily. When we relate, You is not just a "loose bundle of named qualities." You is "neighborless and seamless." The pieces don't disappear; they merge with the larger field…where I meets You.

The pointillism of painter Georges-Pierre Seurat uses small dots of color, meaningless in themselves, to form a beautiful image when taken *in toto.* Similarly, we see the wholeness of a digital photograph, not the millions of pixels that make it up…unless we want to focus on them, of course. Then we're back in I-It.

When we address our partners in their Wholeness, we are reminded of our own as well. There is only Now. The resonance we establish reminds us of our connection to everything.

For my most recent birthday, Micaela escorted me to the Museum of Modern Art and taught me how to see art. Paintings had always been "beautiful objects" for me, and my many trips to museums could be described as "speed-dating the great masters."

Micaela took me under her wing and showed me how to meet a painting as You. Something special happens. All the caring, love, vision, and inspiration that the artist packs into the form re-awakens when encountered as You.

"The single eye of the lion reached out to us"

We stood in front of *The Sleeping Gypsy* by Henri Rousseau and met it as You. I was transfixed. In a museum overflowing with masterpieces, there was only one. The painting took us beyond form and meaning. The single eye of the lion reached out to us from eternity and spoke in the wordless language of the Mystery.

We lasted twenty minutes before we became so blissed-out that we could hardly stand. We had to leave. No more could be taken in that day.

Finding You: Where Are You Now?

It is not our purpose to become each other; it is to recognize each other, to learn to see the other and honour him for what he is.

Herman Hesse

We have seen already that we can amplify Presence by asking:
"Where am I now?" and answering:
"Here I am."
Let's take that to the next level. We move from the one-pointed awareness (NOW!) of Presence to acknowledge and include a partner.
Look your partner in the eye and ask yourself:
"Where are you now?"
And answer:
"Here you are."
Just as in Presence, this question/answer is not to garner information (I-It). It is to engage your partner with caring and attention. There is some urgency to finding You—as if your puppy had wandered off and you are so happy to be reunited. "Here you are!"

Hide-and-seek is the most fundamental game we have (an Indian myth says that everything in the world is God playing hide-and-seek with Her/Himself). This is the spirit of I-You. We hide in the world of objects (and lose ourselves in our thoughts), and then are awakened by an authentic engagement with someone or something in the Present moment. Each time we contact a partner in this way, we share a moment in eternity. We extract ourselves briefly from our worries and fears and meet in a timeless place. Namaste.

Your partner need not return your interest for you to benefit from this. Simply encountering another in this way allows you to move out of your own head and brings you into resonance with You.

This call-and-response is done subvocally with yourself, but if you like, you can do it aloud with someone else who is in on the joke. As a practical matter, however, you will find it easier to implement if it becomes a quick thought used to get you back on track when your mind goes adrift.

"Where are You now?"
"Here You are!"

When we haven't yet made the choice to be present, the mind will busy itself with old patterns until circumstances demand attention. And when we haven't consciously chosen to speak I-You, the mind reverts to an It-trance default setting. The computer runs a familiar subroutine until we are ready to actually relate to someone.

Locating your partner with "Where are You now? Here You are," activates the I-You OS, and we're off to the races.

It bears repeating that I am not locating you as a human *object* by comparing you to other objects in four-dimensional space-time: "That's Joe, five feet to my left in the hallway and it's four-thirty in the afternoon." No, I locate You non-objectively—Now and Here—because Joe ceases to be an object when he is You to my I.

I encounter You, soul-to-soul, from my Wholeness. I am transformed in that moment. You are too, if you choose to meet me in your Wholeness. Time and space only have meaning in reference to You. Clock time is irrelevant. Hours pass in minutes. Minutes take hours. Ego disappears or fades to a vague murmur in the distant background.

He is You and fills the firmament. Not as if there were nothing but he; but everything else lives in his light.

Such authentic encounters are so rare that some people feel threatened to have another person look them in the eye with full attention. Writer Walker Percy wrote, "Why is it that one can look at a lion or a planet or an owl or at someone's finger as long as one pleases, but looking into the eyes of another person is, if prolonged past a second, a perilous affair?"

Eye contact is not absolutely necessary, but it does provide feedback that lets you know you are on the right track. You may be surprised to encounter in that gaze another I seeking You.

There is a road from the eye to the heart that does not go through the intellect.

G. K. Chesterton

Chapter 21

Meeting

All real living is meeting.

Martin Buber

The circumstances of our lives rarely demand that we meet them with full awareness and with our whole being. And when such opportunities arise, we don't always notice.

In the I-It mode there is a buffer...a comfortable intellectual distance between us and the event. When we engage with our full being, however, the ongoing narrative of our lives is interrupted momentarily as we fully immerse in the event. In emergencies, artistic creation, making love, dancing, and sports we find more opportunities to engage fully. There is an uncommon clarity of mind that translates easily into action.

Martial arts demand and train such engagement. Mind, body, and spirit are integrated to allow for the appropriate response to the numerous challenges that present moment by moment. In the internal martial arts especially, skill is directly proportional to one's ability to engage fully. They draw their effectiveness more on mind-body-spirit integration and less on speed, stamina, and strength.

At least that is the theory. But could it be demonstrated?

When I competed in a t'ai chi ch'uan competition called "push hands," I was able to win several national championships in the middleweight class. I then decided to test my skills in the Unlimited division at the U.S. Kuoshu Championships, where I knew I would be at a serious size disadvantage. To my knowledge, it was the first time someone in the U.S. did such a thing. It required a bit of subterfuge to gain entry, and that rankled some of the officials. But since it wasn't expressly forbidden, they let me continue.

When done as a competitive event, the object of push hands is to keep your balance and cause your opponents to lose theirs. Rules vary, but that is the essence. Tournaments attract skilled players and total beginners. You may be matched with someone who thinks push hands is a cross between bad sumo and a schoolyard shoving contest. The litmus test of good players is the relaxed competence they display when they encounter bigger, stronger opponents.

How far do they regress? Can they remain calm and relaxed, yet effective when the action gets heavy?

In many martial arts you objectify your opponent as an "enemy." You learn how to defend against attacks, look for weaknesses, and then attack those targets. This is a perfectly logical, as well as an ancient and proven method for learning self-defense. You train to smite bad guys by pretending your classmates are enemies bent on harm.

And that was the approach I took when I first competed in tournaments. I objectified my opponent as a challenge to overcome. The matches were respectful enough, but many encounters were quite crude and rough. After a few quick victories, though, the novelty of winning for its own sake passed and I felt unsatisfied.

I was winning ugly—displaying intensity and a modest athleticism, but not a high level of t'ai chi skill. This prompted me to change my game radically over the next few years by examining how well I was expressing t'ai chi principles, rather than playing just to win. That meant testing everything about the way I played, including those things that I thought I already did well.

One really surprising development in this process was the growing awareness that my performance improved dramatically when I engaged my opponent in a spirit of cooperation, rather than as an adversary. This was a major departure from my prior training and experience. We became partners (at least to me) in mutual development, rather than obstacles to each other's victory.

The schedule at the Kuoshu didn't allow for much recovery time. I played six matches that afternoon, all against opponents that outweighed me by at least fifty pounds. They were a tough, experienced group with a wide variety of martial skills. Somehow I found myself in the finals against a winner of many championships. Dale was the biggest opponent I ever faced, at 6'6", 275 pounds, so I was giving up a hundred pounds and a lot of strength.

I found that when I engaged my opponent as a partner rather than as an enemy, I was more present and relaxed. I greeted Dale warmly and established a connection right from the start. I smiled and kept my heart open throughout the match, even with some bad calls from one of those disgruntled officials.

Time seemed to distort...elongate. I didn't have to rush. His intentions seemed to be obvious even before they were fully expressed as actions, and this improved my reaction time significantly. My mind was calm and clear even when I was very active. I felt a sense of Wholeness marked by a lack of self-consciousness, as well as an ability to implement my intentions almost instantly. I felt no fear, even though I was overmatched by his size and strength.

Winning that match was a major awakening. Much more important than the victory was the sense that I had broken through to something I didn't yet understand. Such moments of clarity and almost effortless competence were rare at first and left no call back number. I would have to wait until I bumped into them again and then try to recognize what was different.

This was particularly difficult since what I was seeking was a way of being, rather than something I did, and it didn't offer itself up easily to my clumsy tools of inquiry. But I had to follow this will-o'-the-wisp if I was to understand what was going on, and learn how to replicate it. It was a long time before I could find the words to explain what I was doing.

I was meeting my partner as You.

The I-You encounter does not happen in a vacuum. It requires at least one sentient being willing to engage the world and its inhabitants in the present moment. In that moment, I suspends its ongoing narrative and encounters another fully and wholly.

But the narrative returns. The lived life demands it. I-It gives shape and form to relation. It allows us to remember our encounters and learn from them. Meeting includes I-You and I-It: the inside and outside of the encounter.

In the objectless awareness of I-You, there is only NOW. In the object-based awareness of I-It, I can make sense of what is happening. When meeting, we toggle between the two.

Our attention quite naturally gets pulled to stuff we can experience, as well as inferences about the experience. When you hear a song played on the radio, your primary concern is with the sounds you hear and your

responses to it: *Who is that singer? I wish it were louder. That song makes me sad. That was our song. I wonder where she is now. Anne said she was going to Spain. I'd like to go to Spain.* And so on.

As we go deeper into the story, you may not notice the music at all. You probably pay even less attention to the radio waves that make it all possible. They are formless, invisible, and move at the speed of light. More non-stuff than stuff. We only know them by the effects that they have on more substantial things. There isn't much substance to radio waves, yet without them that song on the radio is not happening.

The stuff that we perceive is dependent on the non-stuff that brings it to us. But when we experience something, we focus more on the stuff than the non-stuff. It is so easy to shift into the It-trance that we can easily become oblivious to what is really going on in the Now and Here. All that remains is a story.

Meeting evens it out. We bring as much attention to the non-stuff as we do the stuff. The intangible carrier wave of authentic engagement takes on a bigger role, which enhances our ability to function in the world of the senses.

Meeting in Sports

Sometimes it is easiest to see a principle in action when we observe it in sports. The feedback is fast and the differences between success and failure are small.

Athletes are reminded over and over to meet the ball with baseball bat, tennis racquet, and golf club...and not try to kill it. You practice your stroke until you can smoothly execute it. Then you contact the ball cleanly with your swing. That way the energy of your body movements is transferred efficiently to the object you are hitting.

I couldn't grasp this idea during my youth and my performance suffered accordingly. I considered it my duty to hit a ball as hard as I could, and was usually frustrated by an assortment of whiffs, shanks, slices, and fouls. The rare solid connection only served to validate my poor technique, and encouraged me to try harder.

I didn't understand meeting, or the power and control it could deliver.

When you meet a ball with a bat or club, you are directing your awareness to the point of contact...not just your idea of where the ball might be. Of course, this is easier said than done. Those who master this important principle are able to dazzle us mere mortals with their prestidigitation.

The great baseball player Ted Williams could actually see where his bat met a pitch. That may not sound like a big deal, but it is one of the hardest things to do in sports. He proved it to a skeptical former umpire by coating a bat with tar, then hitting fastballs. The throws were coming at ninety-plus miles per hour and his bat speed was probably in the same range. After swinging, he would call out the location of the contact point. One has to imagine that the moment of impact was incomprehensibly brief, yet Williams could bring enough awareness to that moment to call out the point of contact seven out of ten times.

"Using a grapefruit to find a bullseye"

His vision was the stuff of legend. But that is less important than his willingness to meet the target. South Korean archer Im Dong-hyun set a world record in the 2012 Olympics while legally blind. He fired bullseyes from over seventy-five yards away by tuning into the blurry yellow grapefruit at the center.

To meet is to come together by choice. Of all possible places to put your attention, you bring it to what you want to connect with. You know that when you lose your focus, your performance suffers.

It's not enough to just be present, you have to extend from your position in space and time to contact someone or something. For example, you choose to interact with, say, a golf ball. It just sits there on a tee waiting for you to give it a ride. All you have to do is swing your club like you've done thousands of times. So why do your results vary so widely?

Hook, slice, pop up, shank…or a crisp, satisfying 280-yard drive down the center of the fairway. Unless you are willing and able to bring your awareness exclusively to that dimpled sphere in the Present—and maintain it there for a few seconds—it will be difficult to get all your parts to move in a fluid, coordinated way.

A little adjustment during your backswing, or a premature thought about tracking your ball, and you've broken your connection. Each thought takes you out of the moment you share with the ball and shifts you into experience mode. Then, you and the ball are no longer synchronized.

This is at its worst when an archer experiences "target panic." Something that was easy and predictable becomes a terrifying ordeal. You line up your arrow and your body starts moving on its own. Bad things happen. Your easy groove disappears and now you have to concentrate on just controlling your fine motor skills. Your attention is on your own body now, and your thoughts about it, rather than on meeting your target.

There is an old story where an ant asks a centipede how he knows which leg to move. The centipede thinks about it a long time and then can't remember how to walk.

Contrast this to the athlete in the Zone, who knows exactly what to do—seemingly without thinking. Actually, it only seems like there is no thinking. It's really just dialed way down. There is so much non-objective awareness happening that the thoughts are barely noticeable. The supercomputer has booted up and the individual thoughts are being processed in a blur.

It is a state of seemingly effortless competence, where the doing is its own reward. How do we find this magical Camelot?

We meet.

Meeting is where Martin Buber's incredible vision is fleshed out. It is at once exquisitely transcendent and solidly practical.

In each moment we can choose to interact with someone or something as an It or as a You. Meeting requires both.

You can meet anyone or anything: human, animal, vegetable, mineral, spirit, or thought. When a Van Gogh moves you out of your normal state and you look beyond the vibrant colors and textures to contact that something intangible that reminds you that this artist is something special...you are meeting. When the early morning sun strikes the dew on a spider web and reveals fiery spheres that whisper their unspoken secrets...that is meeting. In your prayers you meet God, a saint, an angel, or your higher Self.

We don't wait for someone to meet us. We go for it. Why? In meeting, we vibrate together and are transformed. And that transforms those we encounter. They may not know it yet, but do it enough and you will see the changes around you.

When a passer-by nods to me and smiles, I can perfunctorily return his greeting and go on about my business, or else I can see the glint in his eye as an opportunity to momentarily recognize and acknowledge his autonomy and identity, independent from mine and all else.

This person is a unique individual who is signaling in some small way that he sees me as deserving of the respect of another sentient being. In our separateness we find inter-subjectivity, and in a moment of mutual respect we transcend that separateness. "Aha! Another sentient being doing whatever it is that sentient beings do! Carry on then!"

In everyone's life, at some time, our inner fire goes out. It is then burst into flame by an encounter with another human being. We should all be thankful for those people who rekindle the inner spirit.

Albert Schweitzer, Nobel laureate

Chapter 22
Finite and Infinite Games

I stretched ropes from steeple to steeple;
garlands from window to window;
gold chains from star to star,
and I dance.

Arthur Rimbaud, French poet

Meeting has two complementary parts.

The first one has been introduced: Encounter your partner with your whole being in non-objective awareness. I-You. This requires Coherence and Presence. You ask, "Where are you now?" and answer, "Here you are!"

The second part establishes what is going on and what we are trying to do. You clarify to yourself what game is being played and if you choose to play it. You ask,

"What game am I playing now?"

and then,

"Is this the game I want to play?"

The word "game" can have a frivolous connotation, but some games can be quite serious indeed. The term can be sometimes off-putting too, because it is often assumed all games must have a winner and a loser. But that is not always the case.

Finite and Infinite Games by James Carse establishes a clear distinction between the two types of games in the title. Carse says that finite games are played within fixed boundaries in order to establish

143

a winner. Soccer and lacrosse, for example, are played according to specific rules that allow us to clearly show who was the dominant team in a particular contest. If the game is to become partner in a law firm and get a corner office with a view, then that is also a finite game. You know when you've won.

Infinite games, by contrast, are not played to establish a winner, but rather to keep the game going. They play with boundaries, not within them.

For example, I practice my martial arts not to be declared the best martial artist or some other title, but to continue to hone my skills and learn new ones. Within that infinite game there are many finite games, such as tournaments won, training sessions where I demonstrated competence in a challenging exercise, or matches where I successfully overcame a

"Infinite games play with boundaries, not within them"

skilled sparring partner. The finite games provide milestones within the larger infinite game, but the real purpose is not to rack up titles; it's the pursuit of mastery.

A loving relationship is an infinite game. Its purpose is to create more love. We make and unmake boundaries to permit even more authenticity in our encounters. The lover is a partner in co-creating new possibilities.

The relationship becomes a finite game, however, when a lover or spouse is a mere acquisition—a trophy—something that shows the world how successful/desirable one is. Or maybe he/she is just a material comfort—sexual, social, financial. The beloved has become an object, something to be possessed.

It can be a fun game to "worship" a partner, to "put them on a pedestal," but those are forms of objectification, too. If that defines the relationship, it has become a finite game: "I worship you." Play that one as often as you like, but don't get stuck there. The infinite game makes and unmakes that structure to create more love. It is a spiritual partnership.

A spiritual partnership continues to grow and develop. Spiritual partners see beyond each other's forms and continue to coax fire from the embers of their souls. I relates to You and invigorates new forms. There is a dynamic balance between experience and relation, objectivity and subjectivity, that never gets old. The world is being created anew with each breath.

Relationship is the form that relating takes—what relating looks like from the outside. There are an infinite variety of forms that relating can assume…and they change in each moment. Some forms follow familiar patterns and are clearly defined: by biology, social conditioning, and personal experience. Your father, my accountant, their football coach—these are names we give to relationships recognizable to many people. They are roles that come with responsibilities and expectations, and can provide the structures that permit true relating to occur…or not.

In the infinite game, structures are shaped by the authentic encounters of participants. The infinite game plays with separation and connection. Boundaries are created and dissolved. A loving relationship contains both the finite and the infinite.

Mindfulness and Games

Mindfulness places attention on what is happening Now. That includes knowing what game is being played. There are games within games within games. Meeting demands that you get up to speed.

It is essential to have a sense of the game being played. This is the I-It part of meeting. We use the intellect to make distinctions that illuminate the "what exactly is it that we are doing?" with this other person or thing. The game may be tacit or explicit, sacred or profane, legal or illegal, cooperative or competitive. We resonate better with each other when we agree to play the same game, but it is not necessary. What is necessary is that there be some understanding of what we are doing together.

Ask yourself:

"What game am I playing now?"

Once you identify the game being played—and it can be as mundane as eating lunch or mowing the lawn—you ask yourself the next question:

Is this the game I want to play now?

For example, Stella is arguing with her mother...again. What game are they playing? Mom feels that if she badgers Stella enough, then Stella will settle down and give her the grandchildren she wants. Stella isn't ready for that right now. She's got other things on her mind.

"Is this the game I want to play?" Stella asks herself. "Not really," she thinks. She knows that nothing good will come of it. So she plays a different game: "Reassuring Mom." She lets

"What game am I playing now?"

Mom know that she has been heard and taken seriously. Yes, she wants children too, and will get right on that when the time is right.

In your workplace you may be playing an infinite game. You want to keep the game going by making the company successful and prosperous. You help others and share your knowledge. That is the essence of good teamwork. People learn to trust each other.

Doreen, however, doesn't get this "infinite game" stuff. She wants to get ahead—fast—and will do whatever it takes to advance her career, even if it means misrepresenting your efforts. Doreen plays the finite game and wants to be "the winner." She doesn't really care about you. This makes you anxious.

You want to meet Doreen exactly as she is. That means clarifying for yourself what game she is playing with you and deciding if you want to play her game. You locate her in the Now and Here with "Where are you now?" "Here you are."

This strips away the story and your anxiety. You are pulled back into the present. You see her for who and what she is. If you don't want to play her game, well, you come up with a better one. Maybe even one Doreen wants to play.

The Game of Creating

As a writer one must be mindful of the game you are playing, moment by moment. It shifts constantly, as ideas present themselves as possibilities. Each sentence…each word…is a game within a game.

I am meeting this book as I write it. That means it is my partner. It comes to me as the unmanifest wishing to be manifest.

It didn't originally come unbidden. I asked for it…prayed for it. When it arrived, a contract was forged. An inspiration came whole and undifferentiated. My job is to convert that numinous potentiality into words that resonate with people.

That is one level of the game.

Sometimes I ask the book for advice. Sometimes I personify it as the Muse. I meet the book as a partner, or the Muse as its representative. When I meet it in that non-objective state, I open to energy and information that is not available to my finite mind. Mark Twain said he only wrote as an amanuensis, a scribe, for thoughts that passed through him. He would shift to another project when the transmissions were interrupted.

For me, the ideas have no form and only as much substance as I grant them, but meet them I must. I must also step back and convert ideas into words—that is, convert the energy patterns that appear in my mind to words on a page. Then I step back again and see how what I just wrote fits in with what preceded it. Is that paragraph what I want right now? Or do I want to go in a different direction?

It is said that all writing is re-writing. That is another level of the game: converting something from non-objective awareness into an object that can be shared with others.

Music is a different kind of game. Beethoven said, "Music is the mediator between the spiritual and the sensual life." It has a universal potential to produce resonance among its listeners and transport them to higher states.

I can hear music…or listen to it…or meet it.

Beethoven's Eighth Symphony plays as I write this. It is not my primary focus right now, but I do hear it. I vibrate together with it even if I am not conscious of that. Occasionally I direct more attention to it and listen for a bit. It has become an object for me. When a particularly juicy section comes up I meet it as a partner...no longer listening from a psychic distance, but immersed. Nothing else matters in this moment. My partner has my full attention.

Music is different when played for people who are there primarily to hear it versus music performed as background for people trying to converse with each other. Different games.

In the former case, musicians and audience engage to mutually create something that both consider important. In the latter, the audience's attention is split between appreciating the music and hearing about their companion's new job or upcoming surgery.

Master musicians know that this is just the nature of the gig and will pour their caring into the music itself. And then there will be those moments when the crowd can't help but pause and really hear what is going down. A great performer meets the audience where it is, and then takes it for a ride.

Music is the one incorporeal entrance into the higher world of knowledge which comprehends mankind but which mankind cannot comprehend.

Ludwig von Beethoven

Chapter 23
Meeting Objects

The old word "observer" simply has to be crossed off the books, and we must put in the new word "participator." In this way we've come to realize that the universe is a participatory universe.

John Wheeler, physicist

Fourteen-year old Arwen sat cross-legged on the floor contemplating a fork. She was surrounded by sixty-odd women and men circled in groups of eight to twelve, all of them holding metal forks. The conference room at a motel in Sedona, Arizona was buzzing with excitement and anticipation as everyone focused on their current mission: use their intention to soften that flatware enough to easily bend and twist it in their hands.

David and Susan, Arwen's parents, were leading the exercise. They enthusiastically instructed the bewildered group in the steps to achieve this improbable task. Only they and their daughter had done this before. To all others in the room it was *terra incognita.* We were there for a

149

yearly gathering to delve into the mysteries of t'ai chi ch'uan and energy healing…and this was certainly a mystery.

Susan dramatically dumped five hundred identical forks in a pile on the floor. They were made of an unidentified alloy, but were stiff enough that only the strongest in the room could bend them (with great effort) under normal circumstances. Everyone was instructed to grab a handful and then form small groups.

I was maybe a little more anxious than the others about this event, because there were several games going on for me. This was my party and it was my idea to get David and Susan to do this. So naturally, I wanted people to have a good time. Of course, I also wanted to "succeed" in the exercise myself. I decided to let things unfold as they would and just enjoy the ride.

My group consisted of a nice blend of martial artists and philosophers. There was a scientific skepticism that permeated our gang, but we were all eager to try.

Five minutes after the group began the activity, the first person called out. In his hand was a bent fork and on his face a broad grin. It was several more minutes before someone else registered a bend. Then another. And another.

Suddenly it kicked in for Arwen too. She made the shift. At first she folded the fork over, surprised and pleased that it would go at all. Even though she had done it before, it seemed new. Then she quickly grabbed another one from the pile of metal and repeated the process, rolling it up the stem and neatly looping it around an imaginary hole. The once rigid metal became very plastic for five to twenty seconds.

During its plastic stage the metal exhibited a range of resistance, but for Arwen it was like shaping a pipe cleaner or soft metal coat hanger. The once straight shaft was transformed into a helix. A fork bent with brute strength will show stress in the metal, but hers were smooth and uniform. It was as if the fork had been heated until soft and then shaped.

Paradoxically, the metal would only yield when you let go of your need for it to do so. You, the fork, and the other people in the room were all one team working together. Information seemed to pass non-verbally and instantly. One person would suddenly bend, then (aha!) another and another would follow suit, the mystery no longer opaque but perhaps just as inexplicable.

It was a group experience, with excitement and wonder replacing confusion and doubt. We reveled in this improbable event. Surprisingly, it was not the big, strong martial artists in the room that were able to "get it" most easily. Some of them were still struggling ten or twenty minutes later. Nor was femininity or youth a guarantee of early success.

We all began the exercise in our It-mind. This was a new challenge… an obstacle to overcome. What Susan and David were asking us to do seemed impossible. Before each of us was a metal fork, rigidly holding onto its rigid metal-ness, defying us mere mortals. Our failures to bend it using muscular strength confirmed that it was indeed a separate object with well-established properties.

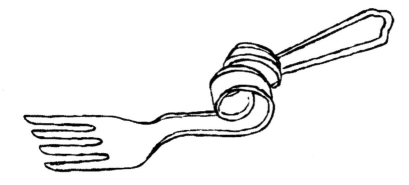

The passage from novice to mastery in any newly learned activity challenges us in many ways. When you first learn to use chopsticks, there is a lot of fumbling around. You feel clumsy and disconnected. You are self-conscious, particularly when you drop a Szechuan dumpling in your lap.

Once you master the tool, however, it becomes part of you. Your intention is expressed instantly through these two pieces of wood. You can now easily pluck a dim sum from the bowl and place it gently in your girlfriend's mouth while telling her how lovely she looks tonight.

Bending presents a different challenge. Rather than learning how to "do" something, it is learning how to "be" differently. We actually shift our state of consciousness to one that is calm, centered, and unified. In this state, heightened and unusual abilities appear. New perceptions become available. The mind is clear and unplagued by fear and internal conflict. Our intuition becomes more accessible.

We feel Whole and Present.

From Wholeness and Presence, we enter into a partnership with this piece of metal alloy. We are not trying to do something to "it," but to resonate together. We ask this seemingly inanimate object to do something with us, to participate together.

We *meet* our partner with just enough It-mind to remember what it is we are doing. But not a lot of awareness is devoted to our narrative. It is the I-You part of meeting that powers this transformation. We are not observers right now; we are participators.

That's when the alchemy happens.

At the meeting.

Warding Off a Bicycle

Maria, a petite grandmother, enjoyed a short break in the park across the street from her midtown office. She saw that traffic had stopped down the block on East 53rd Street in Manhattan. It's a one-way street so she knew it was safe to cross.

It wasn't.

She stepped out past a large double-parked truck and into the path of a speeding delivery bicycle. In the split second before impact, she rounded her left arm to meet the heavy bike with her forearm and stopped it cold. Surprisingly, Maria did not lose her balance. The force of the impact was registered by the metal basket carrying the food: basket and contents were crushed.

Witnesses were alarmed, then relieved to see that she was apparently unharmed. Maria's first response was to ask the bicyclist if he was okay. Flabbergasted and speechless, he quickly exited the scene. She examined her arm and was surprised that there were no cuts or bruises. She shrugged and went back to work.

My wife, Maria, has been studying internal martial arts almost as long as I have. Her instantaneous response came from her t'ai chi training. Stopping a moving vehicle with the back of the forearm is not something that most people would consider doing, and it probably would not have been hers...if her It-mind was in charge. The form she took is not generally a particularly strong muscular connection, but becomes quite powerful when the internal energy is coherent. Just as filling a tire with air transforms it from flexible rubber to a semi-rigid load-carrying structure, animating her arm with coherent energy dramatically and immediately increased her effective power.

In such situations, the "normal" response is to flinch and retreat. That could have resulted in serious injury. Her first impulse was to meet the challenge with Wholeness and Presence. Her years of training made that shift easy. In participatory consciousness, she was able to access energy and information that was unavailable to her It-mind. Perceptions of time and space were altered. Not only were no bones broken, but there wasn't even a bruise or a scratch.

The alchemy of meeting transformed a potentially injurious situation into a harmless event.

It was not just luck that enabled Maria to ward off the speeding bicycle. Chinese internal martial arts teach us how to transform the physical body through conscious interaction. At an age when many have become brittle with osteoporosis, her bones displayed what t'ai chi practitioners call "a steel bar wrapped in cotton." A transformation occurred in the meeting.

Even more dramatically, my t'ai chi classmate, Sol, dispatched a crazed home invader using only his Ward Off. Like Maria, Sol is on the north side of sixty. The attacker broke two knife blades on Sol's forearms without cutting him. He reconsidered his plan at that point and bolted from the apartment.

The Alchemy of Transformation

Objects can be transformed when encountered in participatory consciousness. They are "objects" only because they have been identified as such. Someone brings attention to some small part of the infinite, undifferentiated What-is and experiences it as a separate thing. It is named and included in a story and thus stands apart. It becomes an object.

Buber writes, "But whatever has thus been changed into It and frozen into a thing among things is still endowed with the meaning and destiny to change back ever again." I encounter the object as You and something magical happens. Spirit awakens when I meet You. The object is no longer a thing among things, but my partner in the eternal dance.

Shamans around the world encounter every stick and rock and lightning flash as a conscious collaborator in a world very much alive. As a result, they attune to energy and information that is unavailable to those in the It-trance. Drumming, chanting, ritual are used to get the It-mind out of the way and encourage participation in What-is.

Young children have no problem meeting objects as You. Then they gradually become conversant in the language of It until the It-world subsumes all relating. The wonder of relating fades before the all-consuming power of objectification. They put away childish things.

But even as adults we sometimes talk to things—even when we know they won't talk back. I may see that my tee shot is headed into the lake and I'll implore it to reconsider its path. I wave it over, just in case it can't hear me. The truck driver coaxes his aging F-150 to start on a cold morning. The gambler begs the dice to come up seven.

We educated modern souls know we can't affect a ball in flight by talking to it and trucks and dice don't speak English. Yet we try anyway. We don't even think about it.

Perhaps this relating to objects isn't all silliness or primitive anthropomorphism. We needn't regress to childishness to value it. Something changes dramatically in me when I regard an object as a You, rather than as an It. We resonate with each other in the moment, and that empowers me.

When I pick up a beautiful vase or sculpture with an intention to interact with it rather than just look at it, the psychic distance between us disappears. We become intimate. It's object-ness fades, and I am transformed by our reciprocity.

Try it now. Pick an object and talk to it as if it were sentient. You may feel silly at first, but try anyway. It may help to do it with something you feel more comfortable addressing: a doll, a picture of a person, a car, or a musical instrument. Notice how it feels. Talk to a tree. A computer. You can do it subvocally when you don't want others to think you are daft. The important thing is to establish a real-time connection.

An archer or a dart thrower does it with a target. I meet the space that I occupy when performing martial arts. Something remarkable happens as you move into resonance with the object. You are empowered.

It feels different to be in resonance. You vibrate together. You may take it for granted, but there is a transformation...at least for the moment.

That's what alchemists do. They show that, when we strive to become better than we are, everything around us becomes better, too.

Paulo Coelho, The Alchemist

Chapter 24
Love or Fear

There is no fear in love; but perfect love casteth out fear: because fear hath torment. He that feareth is not made perfect in love.

1 John 4:18, King James Bible

Fear does not abide in the I-You state. It can't. It exists only in the It-mind. This does not mean that fear is not real, or is somehow trivial. It's just that fear can only be recognized by the dependable object-based OS.

To fear anything or anyone, I must separate from it to identify and experience it as a threat somehow. Even when I can't identify it, and the fear is just a sense of foreboding, what I fear is not me. It is something other.

There are physiological sensations that we sometimes associate with fear, and those can pop up anytime. For some of us, any excitement provokes fear and anxiety. It may be a scene from a movie or a particularly suspenseful soccer match. The adrenals are triggered and the It-mind responds by thinking, "Danger!" It labels the event as potentially harmful.

But other people thrive on excitement. The physiological sensations that some call "Danger" are labeled "Fun!" by these people. They want more. One person on the roller coaster wants to stand up, and the person next to her wants to throw up.

In I-You, there are no objects, no story, no threats, and no fear. We resonate with What-is. Buber writes, "As long as the firmament of the

157

You is spread over me, the tempests of causality cower at my heels, and the whirl of doom congeals."

Love embraces What-is. Fear resists What-is. There is a time for both. But when fear dominates our lives, love gets squeezed out. When caught in a web of fear, it is time to be mindful of the game you are playing. If your narrative is one of misplaced fear, then it will color any game you play.

How do I know if my fear is misplaced? What if there really is something to worry about? How can I tell if I'm responding to imagined demons or ghosts long since gone?

Anxiety is a game where I imagine possible futures where things go terribly wrong. I then respond to my scary ideas with physiological responses as if the threats were real and present. This creates more non-coherence, which creates more physiological distress, which causes me to imagine more bad stuff.

It becomes a feedback loop, and to many, it's a way of life. It's the devil we know, comforting in a warped way. The fear-responses are encoded in my body-mind and activated by pre-conscious triggers. At its worst, it becomes trauma or PTSD.

Many of us inherit this way of being in the world from our parents. As children, we accept much of our programming unchallenged. We are not equipped to do otherwise. That programming forms the basis of the unconscious assumptions we carry forward. Just changing my thinking is not enough.

The way out? Play a different game. Often.

What game?

The game of Meeting.

Just because all fear originates in the separation of I and It, that doesn't mean that all I-It is fearful. When done consciously, we are mindful of what is going on and our role in it. We identify the game being played and move into greater resonance with what we think is going on.

But in the It-trance, changing our behavior is not an option. We don't even know that we are in the trance. Permanent, stable change requires awakening from the It-trance again and again.

Meeting then becomes a way of life.

Fear is the cheapest room in the house.
I would like to see you living
In better conditions.

Hafez

Here is one example of meeting an anxiety-producing situation. Don't take it as a script or a formula, but more as a guide. The sequence described is pretty dependable, but may be varied to fit your particular situation.

Pete Gets Anxious

Pete has been at his job for nine years. He hears of potential layoffs in another department. He wonders if he could be next and starts to imagine various scenarios where that could happen, and the consequences of each. As they get more vivid, they produce physical and emotional responses. Pete has trouble sleeping.

Soon, he leaves the realm of "what-if" and becomes certain that something bad is coming down the pipe, even if he doesn't know what. Instead of this being an incentive to perform better, he becomes distracted and irritable. When his boss prods him about an overdue project, Pete gets angry. He is sure the end is nigh.

Clearly, Pete is not really Present with work anymore. He is lost in his imaginary narrative and forgets it is his creation. How does Pete interrupt this downward spiral before it becomes a "crash and burn?" Meeting.

First, he must pull himself out of the loop by getting as coherent as possible. He points and reaches his index fingers and takes some deep breaths until he feels a little calmer. Then does it again until he's calmer still.

Second, he locates himself in the Now and Here, again and again. He frees himself from his self-constructed angst by regaining control of his attention, over and over.

Where am I now?

"Here I am."

He becomes more Present. His mind clears. He doesn't feel like a piñata for his thoughts now. The more Present he is, the more effective he becomes.

Third, Pete becomes more mindful of what is really going on:

What game am I playing now?

"I guess I'm playing the game of arguing with my boss."

Is that the game I want to play?

"Perhaps that's not the smartest play right now. Maybe I should apologize."

What game am I playing now?

"I'm still worried about losing my job. The game is worry."

Is that the game I want to play?

"Worry sure gobbles up a lot of attention. I argue one side, then the opposing view. It never resolves. I work myself into a state and then can't think of anything else. Perhaps I should focus on what I can do effectively."

What game am I playing now?

"I'm clarifying what the actual risks are, so that I can make a rational assessment."

Is that the game I want to play?

"Yes, for the moment. Soon, I would like to get back to creating my career with enthusiasm."

Pete uses this approach to sort through his confused mental state to bring his attention to what really matters to him.

Fourth, he establishes reciprocal partnerships by intentionally going into resonance with What-is. He abandons his fear-based responses by embracing his situation exactly as it is.

This is the hard part, because right now he would really like things to be different. His narrative depicts him as a victim of forces beyond his control. That makes Pete anxious.

There are parts of every situation that cannot be controlled, and some of those are really important. By embracing the event exactly as it is, he can see what those factors are. Pete also sees more clearly what can be changed.

He moves into resonance by locating others in the Present, not as characters in his tired narrative. "Where are You now?" "Here You are." He greets his boss, his co-workers, even his surroundings as You, not as adversaries or tormentors. Even bullies soften when encountered in this way.

Pete is empowered. His anxiety abates. This frees up attention, which allows him to function at a higher level. His co-workers notice his better mood and comment on it. His boss gives him an encouraging review.

Pete has chosen Love over Fear.

Healing Through Meeting

Meeting establishes fertile ground for healing.

My dog Faolan waits patiently at the top of the stairs for me to finish my shower. He's fourteen now, and for a big dog that's Methuselah status. To paraphrase Leonard Cohen, "He aches in the places where he used to play." When he sees me he rolls on his side for his morning Polarity healing session.

To prepare for the session I follow the same sequence Pete used: Establish my energetic coherence by pointing my index fingers, then locate myself in the Present (essential in my seven a.m., pre-coffee state). I become mindful of what game I am playing and meet Faolan as my partner in healing.

The game for me is not "healing Faolan's arthritis." I must detach from outcome. Whatever healing occurs is beyond my power. The game is meeting.

I place my hands on his inflamed joints and connect up by "listening" with my hands. We resonate together and Faolan sighs and closes his eyes. His muscles relax and his breathing gets slower and deeper. The tail wags and he seems content.

I get more explicit feedback from my human clients. We perform more complex maneuvers based on their needs, but the foundation of the healing is still meeting. I create a safe space for them to relax and shift into non-objective awareness. When the autonomic nervous system calms, there is a sense of returning to one's authentic center. In that state, the body-mind is more open to fundamental change.

It starts with meeting, continues with meeting, and ends with meeting.

Meeting Something Bigger Than Me

Even as water becomes one with water,
Fire with fire and air with air,
So the mind becomes one with The Infinite Mind
And thus attains freedom.

Maitri Upanishad

Meeting is a choice to resonate with what is not "me."

That "not-me" can include that which is greater than me: Spirit, God, Oversoul, Higher Power, Brahman, Dao, What-is…whatever we choose to call what transcends and includes anything we can possibly know. We construct our narratives to include the Transcendent, but must render it an It whenever it is named. Religiously observant Jews use *Adonai* ("Lord") when reading the Torah, since they are forbidden to speak the name of God.

When we pray directly to a Supreme Being—not as the most powerful character in our story, but as I to You—we go into resonance at a higher vibration. At its highest level, we experience what some call *unio mystica:* unity consciousness, a sense of perfect union with the All. There is no sense of a separate self, or even an Infinite Other.

Oneness is not an "experience" until we think about it. The labeling turns the unity state into an experience. Prior to the labeling, there is nothing to count. Zhuangzi is credited with saying, "Heaven, earth, and I came along together, and the myriad things and I are one…Myself and my talking make two; talking and the object make three."

In I-You, two does not become one. Two becomes no-thing. There are no objects to count. "Heaven, earth, and I" separate out from What-is only when objectified and labeled. Prior to the labeling, there is only What-is.

Love does not cling to an I, as if the You were merely its "content" or object; it is between I and You. Whoever does not know this, know this with his being, does not know love, even if he should ascribe to it the feelings that he lives through, experiences, enjoys, and expresses. Love is a cosmic force.

Martin Buber

Love isn't a feeling, or something I do. Love is I meeting You in the fullness of being. Love reaches and withdraws, attaches and detaches. It cannot exist without some separation, but cannot exist only in separation.

"Love thrives on the pulsing"

Love thrives on the pulsing. The narrative is the soil where Love roots, but it must reach beyond the story to breathe. Spirit arises when I meets You.

Each time we choose Love, it becomes easier to do. Fear subsides and "the whirl of doom congeals." We invite participation in the lived life, for ourselves and others. Opportunities present themselves unannounced, bearing chocolates and flowers. Strangers smile and nod. Angry dogs roll over on their backs and present their underbellies. Swords are blunted, and guns become bouquets. Where we once met with obstacles, we now find new possibilities.

The World of It is a lonely place, if that is all you know. But there is more.

Turn around. You awaits.

If you make love with the Divine now, in the next life you will have the face of satisfied desire.

Kabir, Indian poet

Chapter 25

The Gongfu of Meeting

Whoever grasps the thousand contradictions of his life,
Pulls them together into a single image, that man, joyful
And thankful, drives the rioters out of the palace.

Rainer Maria Rilke

Meeting sounds pretty easy, doesn't it?

It actually is…when we remember to do it. However, the It-trance is so deeply embedded in our culture that we rarely do…even when fully aware of how much it can improve performance, relationships, and peace of mind. Sub-conscious programming controls most of our attention, and only a determined effort over a long time can tip the balance in favor of participatory consciousness.

Such an effort is called *gongfu* (kung-fu) in Chinese martial arts. Gongfu means something practiced diligently for a long time. (The Chinese character literally means "time and energy.")

The term is commonly applied to martial arts, but anything can have its gongfu. Yoga, chess, carpentry, comedy—they all require practice and time to develop expertise. Gongfu can also mean the degree of mastery you have attained in that activity. It's the knowledge, wisdom, experience, physical skills, confidence, timing—whatever it takes to be exceptional at something. The glue that holds it all together is your commitment and enthusiasm for the subject.

There is no English term that expresses the nuances of gongfu. Your practice is your gongfu. If you achieve a high level of ability you are said to "have gongfu." If you embody the essence of the activity, there will be something intangible that may be recognized with an admiring, "That is gongfu." There is a suggestion in the term gongfu of an ongoing process that is never completed, but continues to spiral upward.

Mastery is the closest translation I have come up with, although it usually connotes a state of accomplishment: attainment of superior skill, or full command of a subject, as in "I have mastered the times tables." We don't usually think of mastery as a process like gongfu.

There is an impulse in all of us to do what we do better. We respect and admire those who elicit goodness, truth, and beauty from the ugly or the mundane. Their creations remind us that we are much more than transient pieces of nerve and sinew subject to the same entropy that leads to death and decay. We all have the potential to engage Life in a dance of transformation that brings us into resonance with our Higher Nature, and break the bonds of time and space. We don't have to be Nobel laureates or brilliant inventors to play this game. It is open to all.

For example, my grandmother baked the best pies I can imagine. Most meals were an austere presentation of overcooked meat, unadorned potatoes, and a limp, boiled vegetable.

Ah, but dessert! Dessert usually consisted of some form of pie: apple, cherry, blackberry, huckleberry (picked by Grandpa and me from wild bushes during our afternoon hike), strawberry, rhubarb (from her garden), peach, pumpkin, or mincemeat (with all hand ground ingredients). Anything that could go in a pie had been joyously employed by this master baker. The formula was simple—fruit baked into an excruciatingly flaky crust. No frills or adornments. Yet somehow what came from that oven trumped any dessert I have had since. Each bite carved new sensory pathways through your nervous system as you struggled to wrap your mind around the miracle in your mouth.

Grandma would have blushed if you called what she did gongfu. To her it was just something she liked doing both for itself and for the appreciation of others. She refined her skills by a lifetime of practice, but most important, she loved what she was doing. It was her gongfu.

Devon's Challenge

Why is gongfu important? What drives some people to excel at what they do? Why are we fascinated with athletes, artists, and performers who push the limits of what is possible? Why do some people feel threatened by the excellence of others? Why do we sometimes fear our own potential? Why do we undermine our own best efforts and intentions? Even when we are ambitious to "do something," how do we know what to do?

This book was largely inspired by a series of conversations with my son, Devon. Then in his mid-twenties, stuck in an unsatisfying job, paying off student loans, he was ready for more, but there was no clear path ahead. Like most of us, he was having trouble getting past some self-imposed limitations, particularly how to move from idea to action in the most effective way.

Devon asked if there was a mental gongfu: a practice that could help us get more out of life by "getting out of our heads." It would help us develop the skills needed to function at a higher level of proficiency in whatever we found interesting.

He said, "With a mental gongfu, you practice so that in the moment of battle, fear will not cloud your mind and you can operate at the height of your game. It would be a set of practices that allow the average person to achieve the same clarity in ordinary action that a warrior looks to achieve in battle."

How do we get out of our own way? How do we avoid the mental lampreys that suck our initiative? Devon saw that what is needed is not just a recipe, but also an ongoing practice that transforms the way we are in the world.

I recognized what he was asking for in my martial arts practice, but I didn't know of a "mental gongfu" that would accomplish the same thing. I have struggled with many of the same issues Devon has and wondered if I could apply some of the hard-won lessons garnered from decades of t'ai chi. Anecdotal opportunities abounded, but what was needed here was to distill the universal wisdom found in the art in a way that was understandable and usable to those who couldn't or wouldn't spend decades studying and practicing it.

There are zillions of "how to" books, videos, and courses to help us learn the fundamentals and intricacies of almost any skill imaginable. But some of us can't make the jump from a book on the shelf to bird feeder in the back yard or cyclotron in the basement. We never got around to learning to walk a tightrope or even half the positions of the Kama sutra.

Students often come to my t'ai chi classes excited to learn those graceful, exotic movements but leave when they find out how much work relaxation really is. Even those of us with extensive training and a record of accomplishment in certain fields find ourselves abandoning them out of confusion and frustration.

Gongfu may seem anachronistic in a world where any time not spent in an unsatisfying job is quickly gobbled up by the lure of television, video games, and web surfing. Drug ads offer biochemical "solutions" to most of life's troubles, and alcohol and recreational drugs help us forget the others. Our ADHD culture promises quick fixes and lots of diversions—instant riches through Powerball or a sweet stock deal, instant fame in a "reality show" or viral YouTube video, instant credibility with a slick public relations move.

Gongfu offers none of this. Its message: You can transform your life through dedicated practice of a worthy activity. The transformation can be complete: physical, mental, spiritual. But it is not gotten on the cheap; it requires that you engage it with heart, dedication, and intelligence. You must physically embody the changes and that takes time and effort.

T'ai Chi and Chinese Internal Martial Arts

Everyone needs to find their own gongfu—something that is intrinsically rewarding for them. If you don't have one, then try various practices until you find something that resonates.

The gongfu of meeting can be part of any practice that you pursue, but it develops best in one that allows you to slow things down and improve control of your awareness. Meditation, yoga, running, walking, dancing—these all fit the bill. Each is enhanced by adding meeting to the process.

As you might have guessed, t'ai chi ch'uan and other Chinese internal martial arts are my preferred route. Diligent practice over time attunes you to qualities of energy, states of consciousness, and extraordinary abilities that are not part of most peoples' awareness. The only way to get beyond pedestrian ability levels is through participatory consciousness. You must engage the practice with your whole being.

The health benefits of t'ai chi are certainly reward enough, but to stop there is to deprive yourself of an amazing spiritual journey. It is often called a "moving meditation" because it helps you to gain control of your awareness while practicing a complex physical exercise. One learns to shift states of consciousness with ease, even when facing stressful challenges.

When you include the gongfu of meeting with your martial arts practice, new doors open. Sure you can practice as an I-It exercise… and most people do. But when you focus on meeting, that is where the woo-woo stuff kicks in.

Why? Because it is only in meeting that we are consciously in the Present. When done as an It-mind exercise, it is an experience. And like any experience, it happens in the past. There is mental distance between me and what I'm doing. That means body, mind, and spirit are out of phase with each other and that generates non-coherence.

In meeting, I am in the Zone, the Flow-state—coherent in mind and body. And that brings me back into Now, where I connect with the Eternal You. Then every action initiates from the Mystery and returns to the Mystery.

This is Body-Mind-Spirit integration.

Energy Healing

The practice of Polarity Therapy and other forms of Energy Healing is a gongfu for me as a practitioner. Sessions are usually an hour of continuous meeting, which is a huge gift for both my client and me. In that time, I must raise my level of Presence way beyond what is called for in most of my activities, and sustain that for long periods.

While not specifically a gongfu for my clients, each session contributes to their own gongfu of meeting. Few of us experience such sustained body-mind-spirit coherence. It poses the question, "What else is possible?" In the altered consciousness of an "ordinary" session, long-held patterns—physical, emotional, mental—are discarded if they no longer serve the individual. They don't even have to be addressed directly. "A rising tide lifts all boats," as the old aphorism says. In this case, heightened coherence is an invitation to the body-mind to shed obviously non-coherent sub-conscious programming.

The scientific foundation of energy healing has been well established by cell biologist James Oschman in his seminal book, *Energy Medicine: The Scientific Basis*. He provides a story that my It-mind can embrace. There is no substitute for knowing what you are doing, and there are specific skills for each modality—acupuncture, homeopathy, shiatsu, for example. But the effectiveness of each is only enhanced by actually meeting the client/patient as co-creator of her own health. She is not an object that you are doing some healing on. True healing is a return to Wholeness, and that requires participation.

And the best healing comes from knowing that you are a full participant in the lived life and embracing all that comes with that. When I find You in the lifeless world of It, the garden bursts into bloom.

I find you in all these things of the world
that I love calmly, like a brother;
in things no one cares for, you brood like a seed;
and to powerful things you give an immense power.

Rainer Maria Rilke

Acknowledgments

Kelly Epperson, my editor, pulled the tractor out of the mud and got the book to the finish line. Our work together has been a master class in writing.

Many thanks to Beatrice Aranow for helping shape the language into its final form with her superb copy-editing.

The great Lawrence LeShan, who led the charge forty years ago with his seminal work *The Medium, The Mystic, and The Physicist,* continues to light the way at age 92 with his brilliant *The Landscapes of the Mind.* Undaunted by health problems that would discourage mere mortals, he continues to write and see patients. It takes a lot of courage to be two generations ahead of your time, and Larry has plenty of that. His encouragement has been priceless.

Jonathan Bricklin, philosopher/tennis partner, has been the Parmenidean whetstone for this work. Our many hours of hair-splitting over our fundamental disagreements have spared the reader some clumsy metaphysical meanderings. Missteps were pounced on and dispatched with a crisp volley.

Nina Deerfield—healer, martial artist, and activist—has been a source of inspiration and support for two decades. Her faith in me has kept me going at some rough points along the way.

My t'ai chi ch'uan students and Polarity clients have shaped me as much as I them. They are too numerous to mention them all, but a special shout out to Dennis McDonald and Stan Kedzierski who were in the first class I ever taught, and are still with me today.

Abdi Assadi, master healer, has been my martial arts training partner for the past twenty-five years. Together and apart, we dove into the maelstrom of Mystery and washed up on distant shores. We always found each other again.

Stephen Watson, insatiable student and generous teacher, has been a joyful ally from the start. We meet in the laughter.

Linda Addison, award-winning poet, has helped to find the Muse and the courage to create.

Ted "Popa Chubby" Horowitz and Dave Keyes, my two favorite musicians, have inspired me with their light and love and song.

Andrew "The Kirtan Rabbi" Hahn shares my love of Buber, music, and martial arts. He sings the One Song and invites all to join him.

My t'ai chi ch'uan teacher, William C. C. Chen, is vibrant and active at eighty-three. He is a living testimony to the negentropy of energetic coherence.

My meditation and martial arts teacher, Fukui Yang, maintains a mailing address in the Mystery and visits there often. He embodies the power of love over fear.

My polarity teacher John Beaulieu walks boldly through dimensions unknown to most and returns bearing gifts.

Devon Barrett, philosopher and novelist, provided the spark to bring this book to life when he asked for a mental gongfu. Before that, it was too impossibly woo-woo to even attempt.

Brian Barrett's heart and wisdom have influenced me since that Easter Sunday forty years ago. It is hard to imagine this book without him. He has made me a better human being.

Micaela Barrett provides the illustrations and cover. She embodies the Rimbaud poem:

I have stretched ropes from steeple to steeple;
garlands from window to window;
gold chains from star to star, and I dance.

Maria Barrett has put up with me for thirty-five years…and it keeps getting better. She holds space for my explorations into *terra incognita*, and I for hers. Life is a lot more pleasant with a partner who sees in you the Eternal You. She makes it all possible.

Resources

These sources were major influences on *Finding You in a World of It*. The first three were indispensible and form the foundation.

Buber, Martin. *I and Thou*. Translated by Walter Kaufman. New York: Scribner and Sons, 1970

Korzybski, Alfred. *Selections from Science and Sanity*. Fort Worth, TX: Institute of General Semantics, 2010

Watson, Burton, trans. *Chuang Tzu: Basic Writings*. New York: Columbia University Press, 1964

The following were also influential and helped shape my thoughts and language:

Berman, Morris. *The Reenchantment of the World*. Ithaca, NY: Cornell University Press, 1981

Carse, James. *Finite and Infinite Games*. New York: The Free Press, 1986

Kodish, Susan Presby and Bruce I. *Drive Yourself Sane: Using the Uncommon Sense of General Semantics*. Pasadena, CA: Extensional Publishing, 2011

Laszlo, Erwin. *Science and the Akashic Field: An Integral Theory of Everything*. Rochester, VT: Inner Traditions, 2004

LeShan, Lawrence. *Einstein's Space and Van Gogh's Sky*. New York: Collier Books, 1982

_____. *Landscapes of the Mind: The Faces of Reality*. Guildford, CT: Erini Press, 2012

_____. *The Medium, the Mystic, and The Physicist*. New York: Penguin Arkana, 1974

Nørretranders, Tor. *The User Illusion: Cutting Consciousness Down to Size.* New York: Viking, 1991

Oschman, James. *Energy Medicine:The Scientific Basis.* Edinburgh, UK: Churchill Livingstone, 2000

Wilber, Ken. *Quantum Questions.* Boston: Shambhala, 2001

Photograph by Michael Ricciardi

Rick Barrett was born in Franklin, Pennsylvania in 1951, the second of eight children, to Dick and Phyllis Barrett.

He has been studying Chinese internal martial arts for thirty-five years and teaching for twenty-five. He won several U.S. national championships in t'ai chi ch'uan push hands, plus the Unlimited weight class at the United World Kung-fu/ Wushu Championships in Orlando (1997). Besides t'ai chi, his internal martial arts include luoxuanzhang, xingyiquan, baguazhang, and yiquan.

Rick practices Polarity Therapy and other forms of energy medicine at his Greenwich Village office in New York. In his healing practice he seeks to empower the individual to true healing: a return to wholeness and full participation in life.

At various times he can be found on the public tennis courts of Staten Island, walking his dog Faolan, or plugging in his Les Paul.

His annual *Tai Chi Alchemy* retreat in Sedona, Arizona explores the possibilities of a "Love-based Martial Art.".

For more information on programs, sessions, or to have Rick speak to your group, contact rb@rickbarrett.net and visit rickbarrett.net

Also by Rick Barrett:
Taijiquan:Through the Western Gate

This book will be a precious resource for all who practice the martial arts and wish to explore the limits of human performance. Demystifying the ancient techniques of taiqjiquan, Rick Barrett leads the reader to draw upon the deep reserves that are always within and around us and to experience phenomena that have for generations passed quietly from teacher to student.

James L. Oschman,
author of *Energy Medicine: The Scientific Basis*

While this book will surely take its just place upon the shelves of every serious Taiji player, what is most rewarding is that the author has similarly found a Gate between the mythic, devoted Taiji player and the rest of us. This tome will be equally at home, and of great value, on the desk of a CEO, in the gym bag of a Special Teams coach, amidst the jumbled paintbrushes of a portraitist, beneath the diploma of your doctor, and as Sunday's second reading.

Stephen Watson,
Member World Wide Martial Arts Hall of Fame

Order your autographed copy at www.rickbarrett.com

$20.00 (includes postage in continental U.S.). Also available for Kindle.